Sixth Workshop on Fact Extraction and VERification (FEVER 2023)

Dubrovnik, Croatia
5 May 2023

ISBN: 978-1-7138-7381-5

Printed from e-media with permission by:

Curran Associates, Inc.
57 Morehouse Lane
Red Hook, NY 12571

Some format issues inherent in the e-media version may also appear in this print version.

Association for Computational Linguistics
209 N. Eighth Street
Stroudsburg, Pennsylvania 18360

Phone: 1-570-476-8006
Fax: 1-570-476-0860

acl@aclweb.org

Additional copies of this publication are available from:

Curran Associates, Inc.
57 Morehouse Lane
Red Hook, NY 12571 USA
Phone: 845-758-0400
Fax: 845-758-2633
Email: curran@proceedings.com
Web: www.proceedings.com

FEVER 2023

The Sixth Fact Extraction and VERification Workshop

Proceedings of the Workshop

May 5, 2023

The FEVER organizers gratefully acknowledge the support from the following sponsors.

Supported by

Introduction

With billions of individual pages on the web providing information on almost every conceivable topic, we should have the ability to collect facts that answer almost every conceivable question. However, only a small fraction of this information is contained in structured sources such as Wikidata; we are therefore limited by our ability to transform free-form text to structured knowledge. There is, however, another problem that has become the focus of a lot of recent research and media coverage: false information coming from unreliable sources.

To ensure accuracy, any content must be verified. However, the volume of information precludes human moderators from doing so. Hence, it is paramount to research automated means to verify accuracy and consistency of information published online and the downstream systems (such as Question Answering, Search and Digital Personal Assistants) which rely on it.

The sixth edition of the FEVER workshop collocated with EACL 2023 aims to continue promoting ongoing research in above area, following on from the first five collocated with EMNLP 2018, EMNLP 2019, ACL 2020, EMNLP 2021, and ACL 2022 and three shared tasks in 2018, 2019, and 2021. This year's workshop consists of 3 oral and 5 poster presentations of accepted papers (54% overall acceptance rate), 12 poster presentations from EACL Findings papers, presentations from 4 invited speakers, as well as a panel discussion with 6 panellists. The workshop is held in hybrid mode with in-person and virtual poster sessions, live-streamed panel discussion, oral presentations, and invited talks.

The organisers would like to thank the authors of all submitted papers, the reviewers, the panelists, and the invited speakers for their efforts, and we are looking forward to next year's edition.

Best wishes,
The FEVER organisers

Organizing Committee

Workshop Organiser

Mubashara Akhtar, King's College London
Rami Aly, University of Cambridge
Christos Christodoulopoulos, Amazon
Oana Cocarascu, King's College London
Zhijiang Guo, Huawei
Arpit Mittal, Meta
Michael Schlichtkrull, University of Cambridge
James Thorne, KAIST
Andreas Vlachos, University of Cambridge

Program Committee

Program Committee

Pepa Atanasova, University of Copenhagen
Daniel Guzman Olivares, Autonomous University of Madrid
Pride Kavumba, Tohoku University
Pietro Lesci, University of Cambridge
Irene Li, Yale University
Adian Liusie, University of Cambridge
Christopher Malon, NEC Laboratories America
Sandeep Mavadia, Amazon
Mitch Paul Mithun, University of Southern California
Marco Mori, Banca d'Italia
Jingcheng Niu, University of Toronto
Allen G Roush, Oracle
Mohammed Saeed, EURECOM
Jodi Schneider, University of Illinois, Urbana Champaign
Dominik Stammbach, ETH Zürich
Md Zia Uddin, SINTEF Digital
Francielle Vargas, Universidade de São Paulo
Amelie Wuehrl, University of Stuttgart
Zhangdie Yuan, University of Cambridge

Invited Speakers

Iryna Gurevych, TU Darmstadt
Dirk Hovy, Bocconi University
Tom Stafford, University of Sheffield
Lucy Lu Wang, University of Washington

Panellists

Isabelle Augenstein, University of Copenhagen
Mohit Bansal, UNC Chapel Hill
Christopher Guess, Duke University
Preslav Nakov, MBZUAI
Tom Stafford, University of Sheffield

Table of Contents

Rethinking the Event Coding Pipeline with Prompt Entailment
Clément Lefebvre and Niklas Stoehr 1

Hierarchical Representations in Dense Passage Retrieval for Question-Answering
Philipp Ennen, Federica Freddi, Chyi-Jiunn Lin, Po-Nien Kung, RenChu Wang, Chien-Yi Yang, Da-shan Shiu and Alberto Bernacchia 17

An Entity-based Claim Extraction Pipeline for Real-world Biomedical Fact-checking
Amelie Wuehrl, Lara Grimminger and Roman Klinger 29

Enhancing Information Retrieval in Fact Extraction and Verification
Daniel Guzman Olivares, Lara Quijano and Federico Liberatore 38

World Knowledgein Multiple Choice Reading Comprehension
Adian Liusie, Vatsal Raina and Mark Gales 49

BEVERS: A General, Simple, and Performant Framework for Automatic Fact Verification
Mitchell DeHaven and Stephen Scott 58

An Effective Approach for Informational and Lexical Bias Detection
Iffat Maab, Edison Marrese-Taylor and Yutaka Matsuo 66

Program

Friday, May 5, 2023

09:00 - 09:45 *Keynote Talk: Iryna Gurevych*

09:45 - 10:30 *Contributed Talks*

Hierarchical Representations in Dense Passage Retrieval for Question-Answering
Philipp Ennen, Federica Freddi, Chyi-Jiunn Lin, Po-Nien Kung, RenChu Wang, Chien-Yi Yang, Da-shan Shiu and Alberto Bernacchia

Enhancing Information Retrieval in Fact Extraction and Verification
Daniel Guzman Olivares, Lara Quijano and Federico Liberatore

BEVERS: A General, Simple, and Performant Framework for Automatic Fact Verification
Mitchell DeHaven and Stephen Scott

10:30 - 11:15 *Coffee break*

11:15 - 12:00 *Keynote Talk: Lucy Lu Wang*

12:00 - 12:45 *Poster session*

Rethinking the Event Coding Pipeline with Prompt Entailment
Clément Lefebvre and Niklas Stoehr

An Entity-based Claim Extraction Pipeline for Real-world Biomedical Fact-checking
Amelie Wuehrl, Lara Grimminger and Roman Klinger

World Knowledgein Multiple Choice Reading Comprehension
Adian Liusie, Vatsal Raina and Mark Gales

An Effective Approach for Informational and Lexical Bias Detection
Iffat Maab, Edison Marrese-Taylor and Yutaka Matsuo

Non-archival: *Prompting for explanations improves Adversarial NLI. Is this true? {Yes} it is {true} because {it weakens superficial cues}*
Pride Kavumba, Ana Brassard, Benjamin Heinzerling, and Kentaro Inui

EACL Findings: *Implicit Temporal Reasoning for Evidence-Based Fact-Checking*
Liesbeth Allein, Marlon Saelens, Ruben Cartuyvels and Marie-Francine Moens

EACL Findings: *Topic Ontologies for Arguments*
Yamen Ajjour, Johannes Kiesel, Benno Stein and Martin Potthast

EACL Findings: *Entity-Aware Dual Co-Attention Network for Fake News Detection*
Sin-Han Yang, Chung-Chi Chen, Hen-Hsen Huang and Hsin-Hsi Chen

EACL Findings: *Relation Extraction with Weighted Contrastive Pre-training on Distant Supervision*
Zhen Wan, Fei Cheng, Qianying Liu, Zhuoyuan Mao, Haiyue Song and Sadao Kurohashi

EACL Findings: *Crawling The Internal Knowledge-Base of Language Models*
Roi Cohen, Mor Geva, Jonathan Berant and Amir Globerson

EACL Findings: *Selective-LAMA: Selective Prediction for Confidence-Aware Evaluation of Language Models*
Hiyori Yoshikawa and Naoaki Okazaki

EACL Findings: *PubMedCLIP: How Much Does CLIP Benefit Visual Question Answering in the Medical Domain?*
Sedigheh Sarah Eslami, Christoph Meinel and Gerard de Melo

EACL Findings: *Open Information Extraction with Entity Focused Constraints*
Prajna Upadhyay, Oana Balalau and Ioana Manolescu

EACL Findings: *Detecting Contextomized Quotes in News Headlines by Contrastive Learning*
Seonyeong Song, Hyeonho Song, Kunwoo Park, Jiyoung Han and Meeyoung Cha

EACL Findings: *Active PETs: Active Data Annotation Prioritisation for Few-Shot Claim Verification with Pattern Exploiting Training*
Xia Zeng and Arkaitz Zubiaga

EACL Findings: *Reading and Reasoning over Chart Images for Evidence-based Automated Fact-Checking*
Mubashara Akhtar, Oana Cocarascu and Elena Simperl

Friday, May 5, 2023 (continued)

	EACL Findings: *Double Retrieval and Ranking for Accurate Question Answering* Zeyu Zhang, Thuy Vu and Alessandro Moschitti
12:45 - 14:15	*Lunch Break*
14:15 - 15:00	*Keynote Talk: Dirk Hovy*
15:00 - 15:45	*Keynote Talk: Tom Stafford*
15:45 - 16:30	*Coffee break*
16:30 - 18:00	*Panel Discussion: 6 years of FEVER workshops - how far have we come? With Isabelle Augenstein, Mohit Bansal, Christopher Guess, Preslav Nakov, and Tom Stafford.*

Rethinking the Event Coding Pipeline with Prompt Entailment

Clément Lefebvre*
Swiss Data Science Center
clement.lefebvre@datascience.ch

Niklas Stoehr*
ETH Zürich
niklas.stoehr@inf.ethz.ch

Abstract

For monitoring crises, political events are extracted from the news. The large amount of unstructured full-text event descriptions makes a case-by-case analysis unmanageable, particularly for low-resource humanitarian aid organizations. This creates a demand to classify events into event types, a task referred to as event coding. Typically, domain experts craft an event type ontology, annotators label a large dataset and technical experts develop a supervised coding system. In this work, we propose PR-ENT[1], a new event coding approach that is more flexible and resource-efficient, while maintaining competitive accuracy: first, we extend an event description such as "Military injured two civilians" by a template, e.g. "People were [Z]" and prompt a pre-trained (cloze) language model to fill the slot Z. Second, we select suitable answer candidates Z^* = {"injured", "hurt"...} by treating the event description as premise and the filled templates as hypothesis in a textual entailment task. In a final step, the selected answer candidate can be mapped to its corresponding event type. This allows domain experts to draft the codebook directly as labeled prompts and interpretable answer candidates. This human-in-the-loop process is guided by our codebook design tool[2]. We show that our approach is robust through several checks: perturbing the event description and prompt template, restricting the vocabulary and removing contextual information.

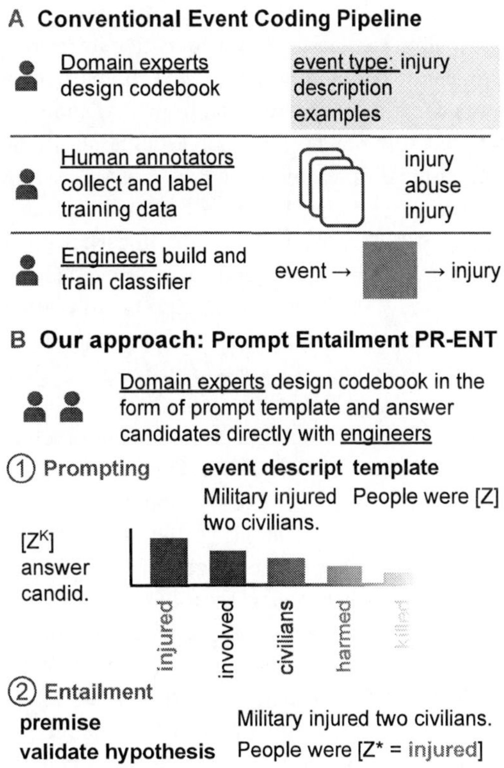

Figure 1: **(A)** The conventional event coding pipeline involves many hand-overs between involved stakeholders and is strictly tailored to the event ontology. **(B)** Our approach combines prompting and textual entailment to perform flexible, unsupervised event coding.

1 Introduction

Decision-makers in politics and humanitarian aid report a growing demand for comprehensive and structured overviews of socio-political events (Lepuschitz and Stoehr, 2021). For this purpose, news papers are automatically screened for event mentions, a task referred to as *event detection* and *extraction*. The sheer amount of extracted, full-text event descriptions day-to-day is impossible to be parsed by humans, especially when limited by scarce financial and computational resources.

Event coding seeks to automatically classify event descriptions into pre-defined event types. Event coding is conventionally approached via a multi-step pipeline as shown in Fig. 1A. It incurs large costs in terms of human labor and time. We sketch out this pipeline expressed in *human intelli-*

*authors contributed equally
[1]https://huggingface.co/spaces/clef/PRENT-Demo
[2]https://huggingface.co/spaces/clef/PRENT-Codebook

Proceedings of the Sixth Fact Extraction and VERification Workshop (FEVER), pages 1–16
May 5, 2023 ©2023 Association for Computational Linguistics

gence tasks (HITs)[3] (ul Hassan et al., 2013).

As a first step, an *event ontology* is defined in terms of a codebook. Codebook development requires multiple domain experts (Goldstein, 1992) spending up to 200 HITs. The initial development phase of the widely-used Conflict and Mediation Event Observations (CAMEO) (Schrodt, 2012) codebook reports a 3-year initial development phase. Next, context-relevant event descriptions need to be collected to serve as training data. This often requires paid access to online newspaper distribution services and data collection infrastructure, estimated at 200 HITs. Next, human annotators need to be recruited and trained to annotate data according to the codebook accounting for another 200 HITs. Finally, a machine-based coding system needs to be developed, trained and validated, costing another 200 HITs. In earlier days, systems were dictionary- and pattern- based (King and Lowe, 2003; Norris et al., 2017), while more recently machine learning-based approaches have gained momentum (Piskorski and Jacquet, 2020; Olsson et al., 2020; Hürriyetoğlu, 2021).

In total, the conventional event coding pipeline amounts to roughly 800 HITs. This development cost is often not bearable by non-profit / non-governmental organizations in the humanitarian aid sector. Moreover, the process requires multiple hand-overs between workers of different background which leads to errors, misunderstanding and delays. It is also important to highlight that the developed coding system is specifically tailored to a fixed event ontology. Any post-hoc changes of event types or even a different dataset incurs huge costs. In practice, event types frequently change and even vary widely between different divisions of the same organization.

To address these shortcomings, we present a new paradigm for highly adaptive event coding. Based on our method illustrated in Fig. 1B, domain experts are able to work directly with an interactive coding tool to design a codebook. They express event types by means of prompt templates and single-token answer candidates. For automated coding, a pre-trained language model is prompted to fill in those answer candidates taking a full-text event description as an input. Since prompting can be noisy (Gao et al., 2021), we propose filtering answer candidates based on textual entailment. Specifically, our contributions are as follows: (1) We propose a methodology combining prompting (§3.1) and textual entailment (§3.2) for event coding, termed PR-ENT. (2) We thoroughly evaluate this paradigm based on three aspects: accuracy (§4.1), flexibility (§4.2) and efficiency (§4.3). (3) We present two online dashboards: (a) A demo of the PR-ENT coding tool. (b) An interactive codebook design tool that guides the codebook design by presenting accuracy validation in a human-in-the-loop manner (§6).

[3]In our formulation, one HIT corresponds to roughly one hour of low-skill work by a single person such as reading and labeling single-sentence event descriptions. Our estimations are based on practical experience in working with domain experts and human annotators in the field of political event coding and serve the purpose of providing a very approximate quantification of required resources and labour.

2 Event Data and Types

We consider a subset of the Armed Conflict Location and Event Data (ACLED) (Raleigh et al., 2010) dataset. It is widely-used and has large coverage of political violence and protest events around the world. Each event is human annotated with a short description, its event type and additional details such as the number of fatalities and actor and targets. The event types are based on ACLED's own event ontology which distinguishes 6 higher-level and 25 lower-level event types. Some event types are easily separable (e.g. *protests* vs *battles*), while others are harder to distinguish semantically (e.g. *protests* vs *riots*) (see Fig. 9 in the appendix).

We sample 4000 ACLED events (3000 for training, 1000 for testing) in the African region while maintaining the event type distribution of the full dataset (see Fig. 9). We remove empty event descriptions and annotator notes (e.g. "[size: no report]"). In Fig. 8 in the appendix, we present statistics of the test set, showing different aspects of linguistic complexity. In §4.2, we consider the Global Terrorism Dataset (GTD) (LaFree and Dugan, 2007) to study the effect of domain shift.

3 Entailment-based Prompt Selection

Our approach, PR-ENT, represents a real-world use case of prompting and textual entailment to code event descriptions $e \in \mathcal{E}$ into event types $y \in \mathcal{Y}$ as shown in Fig. 1B.

3.1 Prompting

Methodological Approach. In traditional supervised learning, a model is trained to learn a mapping between the input e and the output class y. *Prompting* (Liu et al., 2021) is a learning paradigm making use of (cloze) language models that have been trained to predict masked tokens within text.[4] Prompt-based learning transfers this capability to perform classification in the following way:

We extend each *event description* $e \in \mathcal{E}$ by a *template* $t \in \mathcal{T}$ to form the input $\langle e, t \rangle \in \mathcal{E} \times \mathcal{T}$. Each template contains a *masked slot* Z, e.g. "This event involves [Z]", "People were [Z]".[5] The language model takes $\langle e, t \rangle$ as input and returns an *output distribution* of probabilities over the *answer vocabulary* $\mathcal{Z}$. Each token $z_{e,t} \in \mathcal{Z}$ can serve as a potential slot filler to $Z = z_{e,t}$. However, we only consider the top k most probable *answer candidates* $z^k_{e,t} \in \mathcal{Z}^K_{e,t}$. $\mathcal{Z}$ can be a constrained subset $\mathcal{Z}_t$ that only features a template-related answer vocabulary to increase interpretability as pointed out in §5. We discuss how to map answer candidates to event types in §4.1.

Implementation Details. We discuss the design of templates and constrained answer vocabularies resulting in a codebook (Tab. 7) in §6. In particular, we prompt DistilBERT-base-uncased (Sanh et al., 2020), a *distilled* version of the BERT model which is more computationally efficient at the cost of a small performance decrease. For each prompt, we consider the $K = 30$ most probable tokens as the set of answer candidates $\mathcal{Z}^K_{e,t}$. Ideally, we select a larger set, but performance gains are minimal while computational costs increase in subsequent steps.

3.2 Textual Entailment

Limitations of Prompting. Prompting yields event-related tokens for event coding, but comes with challenges. There is no guarantee that a prompted answer candidate $z^k_{e,t} \in \mathcal{Z}^K_{e,t}$ is suited to represent an event. Answer candidates may be semantically unrelated as shown in Fig. 2. To address this shortcoming, we propose filtering $\mathcal{Z}^K_{e,t}$ via textual entailment. Textual entailment, or natural language inference (NLI) (Fyodorov et al., 2000; Bowman et al., 2015) can be framed as the following task: Given a "premise", verify whether a "hypothesis" is true (entailment), false (contradiction), or undetermined (neutral). It has been evaluated as a popular method for performing text classification (Wang et al., 2021).

[4]"Cloze" pertains to filling in missing tokens not necessarily uni-directional left-to-right, but anywhere in a string.

[5]The first prompt template is intended to provide a one-word summary of the event. For the second template, we expect a verb describing the actions undertaken by the actor or a verb that describes what happened to the target.

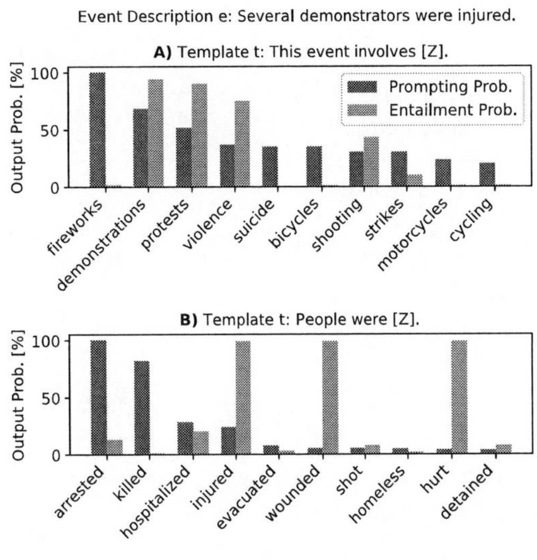

Figure 2: Given the event description "Several demonstrators were injured." and two templates **(A)** and **(B)**, prompting alone can yield tokens that fit syntactically but not semantically (blue bar). In contrast, filtering prompted answer candidates via textual entailment leaves us with tokens more closely related to the event (orange bar). To this end, we treat the event description as premise and the filled template as hypothesis.

Selecting Entailed Answer Candidates. We consider the event description e as premise and the template t' filled with a prompted answer candidate as hypothesis. For example, given the premise "Two bombs detonated...", we automatically construct hypotheses "This event involves $[z^k_{e,t}] \in \mathcal{Z}^K_{e,t} = \{$explosives, civilians...$\}$", see Tab. 1. We pass the concatenation of the premise and hypothesis to RoBERTa-large-mnli (Liu et al., 2019). If the model finds premise and hypothesis to be entailed, then the prompted answer candidate $z^k_{e,t}$ is considered an *entailed answer candidate* $z^*_{e,t}$ (e.g. $z^*_{e,t}$ = explosives). We combine the categories "neutral" and "contradiction" into one since we are interested in a hypothesis being entailed or not.

This means, PR-ENT has two hyperparameters: the top K answer candidate tokens yielded by the prompting step and the acceptance threshold in the entailment step that governs whether an answer candidate is kept. We empirically analyse the effect of both hyperparameters on the final F1 classification score in Fig. 5. In Fig. 5A, we verify that considering the top 30 answer candidate tokens leads to good performance on average. Further, we find a suitable threshold of 0.5 on the entailment model's output probability in Fig. 5B.

Event Description + Template $\langle e, t \rangle$	Answer Candidates $z^k_{e,t}$	Entailed Answer Candidates $z^*_{e,t}$
Several demonstrators were injured. + People were $[Z]$.	arrested, killed, hospitalized, injured, evacuated, wounded, shot, homeless, hurt, detained	injured, wounded, hurt
Several demonstrators were injured. + This event involves $[Z]$.	fireworks, demonstrations, protests, violence, suicide, bicycles, shooting, strikes, motorcycles, cycling	demonstrations, protests, violence
The sponsorship deal between the shoes brand and the soccer team was confirmed. + This event involves $[Z]$.	sponsorship, nike, sponsors, fundraising, cycling, advertising, charity, donations, concerts, competitions	sponsorship, sponsors, advertising, competitions

Table 1: We prompt a language model based on an event description e and template t with slot Z. We keep only those prompted answer candidates $z^k_{e,t} \in \mathcal{Z}^K_{e,t}$ entailed in a subsequent textual entailment task $z^*_{e,t} \in \mathcal{Z}^*_{e,t}$.

4 Evaluation: Event Classification

We compare PR-ENT against the conventional event coding pipeline in an evaluation along three dimensions: accuracy, flexibility and efficiency.

4.1 Accuracy

So far we have not discussed how to map entailed answer candidates $z^*_{e,t} \in \mathcal{Z}^*_{e,t}$ onto event types $y \in \mathcal{Y}$. We choose to do *hard* prompting, as opposed to *soft* prompting. This means, tokens in $\mathcal{Z}^*_{e,t}$ are mapped onto event types y via a simple linear transform $y = f(z^*_{e,t})$. When f is the identity function, no additional mapping is needed (§4.2). Hard prompting allows defining event types, i.e. an event ontology, in terms of interpretable answer candidates. As an example, we present an interpretable event ontology in Tab. 7 in the appendix. We use it to classify "lethal" and "non-lethal" event as explained in §4.2. Generally, we observe a trade-off between accuracy and interpretability. We want different sets of entailed answer candidates to uniquely define different event types at a high accuracy. At the same time, we require the set to be limited to a few, interpretable tokens only, that are highly representative for the event type. In the following, we learn a shallow mapping between $\mathcal{Z}^*_{e,t}$ and the 6 high-level event types $\mathcal{Y}$ provided by the ACLED event ontology as ground truth.

Baselines and Ceilings. As baselines, we consider *bag-of-words* (BoW) and GloVe (Pennington et al., 2014) embeddings of event descriptions. Embeddings are mapped onto event types via logistic regression (LR). Further, we contrast our PR-ENT with a prompting-only (PR) approach also using logistic regression as a classification layer. As a ceiling model, we consider DistilBERT fine-tuned in a sequence classification task.

Model	Accuracy	F1 Score
BoW + LR	80.5	77.1
GloVe + LR	78.5	74.6
Random Tokens + BoW + LR	77.1	72.2
PR + BoW + LR	82.9	80.8
PR-ENT + BoW + LR	85.1	83.7
DistilBERT	**87.1**	**86.0**

Table 2: Classification of 6 event types in the ACLED dataset. As expected, DistilBERT performs best as it is fine-tuned specifically on this classification task. Our approach PR-ENT is more ad-hoc and does not fall far behind. The additional entailment step reduces noise compared to the prompting-only approach PR. On top of the two standard baselines using BoW and GloVe, we introduce an additional baseline where we select 10 random tokens from $\mathcal{Z}^K_{e,t}$ for each $\langle e, t \rangle$. Compared to all baselines, PR-ENT performs better.

Our Approach PR-ENT. To evaluate our approach, we only consider the template "This event involves $[Z]$" and construct a BoW feature matrix by extending the event descriptions e with the entailed answer candidates $z^*_{e,t}$. The resulting feature matrix serves as input to logistic regression. We report classification results in Tab. 2 and find that PR-ENT is only outperformed by the supervised, fine-tuned DistilBERT ceiling, but performs better than all baselines.

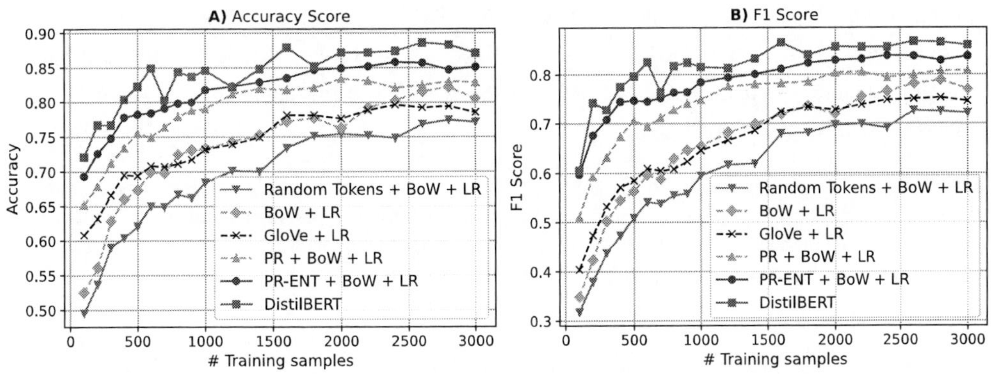

Figure 3: Comparison of the different classification approaches on a varying number of training instances. Our approach PR-ENT shows better performance in terms of accuracy and F1 Score than the baseline models at all points. At the same time, it does not lack far behind the fine-tuned DistilBERT ceiling model, which is however less flexible and resource-intensive. PR refers to prompting-only, BoW to bag-of-words and LR to logistic regression. The baseline "random" consists of sampling 10 random tokens from $\mathcal{Z}^K_{e,t}$ for each $\langle e, t\rangle$.

4.2 Flexibility

We explore the flexibility of PR-ENT along 3 dimensions: changing the number of training instances, omitting the shallow mapping for classification and switching to another dataset.

Number of Training Instances. As can be seen in Fig. 3, our approach shines at classifying event types if only few training instances are given. PR-ENT shows better performance than all baseline approaches introduced in §4.1. At the same time, it is not far behind the fine-tuned DistilBERT ceiling model.

Removing the Shallow Mapping. We may remove the requirement of adding a shallow mapping $y = f(z^*_{e,t})$. Therefore, we predict if an event is "lethal" ($y = 1$) or not ($y = 0$) based on its description. We use PR-ENT to generate entailed answer candidates $\mathcal{Z}^*_{e,t}$ based on the template "People were $[Z]$.". If $Z =$ "killed" $\in \mathcal{Z}^*_{e,t}$ then $y = 1$. We compare PR-ENT against fine-tuned DistilBERT trained on 100 samples and present results in Tab. 3. PR-ENT is competitive against DistilBERT, even outperforming it in this setting. Moreover, while the prompting-only approach (PR) has very high recall, it lacks precision. The additional entailment step in PR-ENT balanced this out, yielding a high F1 score.

Model	F1 Score	Precision	Recall
PR-ENT	**91.6**	**85.3**	98.8
Prompting Only	50.6	33.9	**100**
DistilBERT	84.1	76.5	93.4

Table 3: Binary classification of "non-lethal versus lethal" events based on ACLED's fatality counts. In PR-ENT and prompting-only PR, we code "lethal" if "killed" is present in the answer candidates of "People were $[Z]$.". We observe the added value of the entailment step in the increase in precision. PR-ENT outperforms DistilBERT trained on 100 data instances and tested on 1000 event descriptions.

Domain Shift. We scrutinize the robustness of PR-ENT by switching to another dataset. We repeat the binary "lethal versus non-lethal" classification task on the *Global Terrorism Database* (GTD) (LaFree and Dugan, 2007). The results in Tab. 4, again suggest high performance of PR-ENT.

Model	F1 Score	Precision	Recall
PR-ENT	**96.3**	**94.0**	98.8
Prompting Only	67.3	50.7	**100**
DistilBERT	93.4	89.9	97.2

Table 4: Binary classification of "non-lethal versus lethal" based on the Global Terrorism Database (GTD). PR-ENT and prompting-only PR predict "lethal" if "killed" is prompted from "People were $[Z]$.". PR-ENT outperforms DistilBERT trained on 100 data instances and tested on 1000 event descriptions.

4.3 Efficiency

In §1, we estimated the cost of 800 human intelligence tasks (HIT) for the conventional event coding pipeline. We perform the same estimation exercise for our approach: domain experts design suitable

Perturbation Type	Paraphrase		Remove Stop Words		Remove Entities		Duplication	
Model Type	PR	PR-ENT	PR	PR-ENT	PR	PR-ENT	PR	PR-ENT
1 Perturbation	0.33	**0.14**	0.22	**0.15**	0.15	**0.08**	0.18	**0.09**
2 Perturbations	0.34	**0.18**	-	-	-	-	0.28	**0.16**

Table 5: Average Jensen-Shannon distance across 1000 event descriptions. We conduct 4 perturbation tests: paraphrasing the template, removing stop words from the event description, replacing named entities by a placeholder, and duplicating words in the template. PR-ENT is more robust than PR: in all cases, the distance between the output distributions based on the non-perturbed and perturbed input is smaller.

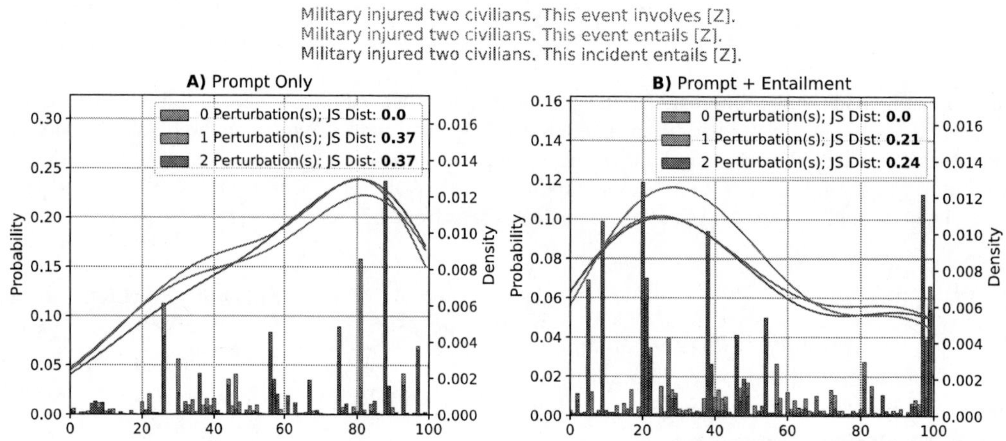

Figure 4: We compare prompting-only PR and our approach PR-ENT when perturbing the input $\langle e, t\rangle$. PR-ENT is more robust to perturbations as indicated by a lower Jensen-Shannon distance between the output distributions over answer candidates based on non-perturbed and perturbed input. PR is highly sensitive to template phrasing. X-label represents the top 100 most frequent tokens from 1000 prompts.

templates and answer candidate sets in a trial and error fashion as elaborated in §6. We estimate total development costs at about 300 HITs, which makes it particularly feasible for small teams with few resources such as non-governmental organizations in humanitarian aid. Overall, our approach requires fewer people and consequently fewer hand-overs. Moreover, it is not tied to a specific event ontology and more flexible for changing event types.

5 Ablation Study

5.1 Perturbation Tests

Our approach is not tailored to a specific event ontology, but to a language model. Any performance gains on these models, such as the recently published ConfliBERT (Hu et al., 2022), will impact our pipeline. A crucial consideration is the presence of biases within language models. In some settings, biases may even be desirable inductive priors, but should at least be known.

We measure the sensitivity of the prompted model's output distribution to changes in the input. To this end: we select a fixed answer vocabulary $\mathcal{Z}_t$ of 100 tokens by taking the most frequent tokens yielded by the prompted model across 1000 event descriptions. We observe the output distribution over tokens in $\mathcal{Z}_t$ before and after perturbing the input $\langle e, t\rangle$. Finally, we measure the difference between the two output distributions in terms of Jensen-Shannon (JS) distance. We show the results of the following four perturbation settings in Tab. 5:

(1) Paraphrasing Two prompt designers could come up with paraphrased templates. In Fig. 4, we show that the additional entailment step makes PR-ENT more robust to perturbations in the template as opposed to prompting only.

(2) Stop Word Removal We remove stop words from the event description to test PR-ENT on non-grammatical text.

(3) Context Removal We remove all named entities in event descriptions and replace them with placeholder tokens such as "organizations" and "locations". This verifies that PR-ENT is less prone to latching onto context instead of content.

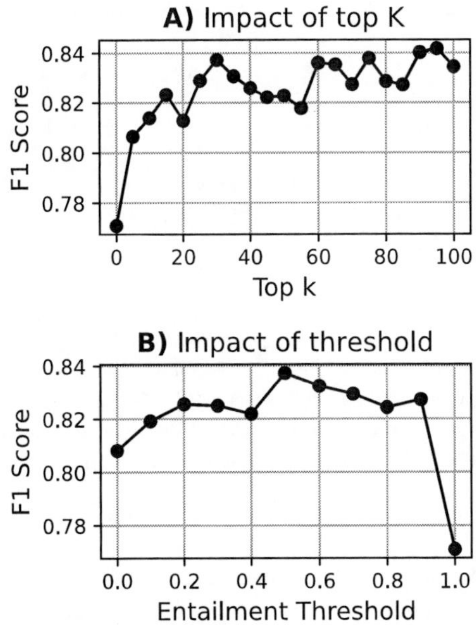

Figure 5: Impact of different parameters of our pipeline on ACLED classification. **(A)** F1 score versus the maximum number K of allowed answer candidates; $K = 0$ means that only the event description is used in the classification. **(B)** F1 score versus entailment threshold; the threshold governs if a hypothesis is entailed with the premise or not, a threshold of 0 means that all prompted answer candidates are considered. A threshold of 1 means only the event description is considered.

(4) Duplication We duplicate some words in the template. Specifically, we test the 3 prompts: "This event involves $[Z]$", "This event event involves $[Z]$", "This event event event involves $[Z]$".

5.2 Comparing Coded Event Time Series

Using PR-ENT, we construct a codebook (Tab. 7) to code ACLED event descriptions without the need of a shallow mapping. We use this codebook to code events that took place in Mali (Fig. 6) and Ethiopia (Fig. 6) between 2009 and 2021. This allows comparing time series of event types between our approach and ACLED's coding. We find that both codings yield very similar time series in which the positioning of spikes align. Yet, the spikes in the PR-ENT time series are higher / steeper indicating that more events are detected. This may be attributed to two reasons: firstly, PR-ENT is potentially more granular and has higher recall. Secondly, PR-ENT is not limited to coding only one event type per event description as ACLED is. For example, the following event description in ACLED (anonymized) is coded as Armed Clash but contains several possible event types (Armed Clash, Killing, Kidnapping, Property Destruction, Looting): "[...] The militants clashed with [ORG], and killed one [ORG] and a civilian driver, abducted one person, burned a vehicle and seized livestock."

5.3 Qualitative Error Analysis

We perform a qualitative error analysis of our proposed method. Within the ACLED data, there are many event descriptions containing mentions of past events (e.g. "Protests over the killing of the journalist [NAME] shot dead on Monday at his home by armed bandits."). Our method, and in fact, any supervised classifier, may have difficulties recognizing event co-references. Another frequent error is due to ACLED event type definitions. For instance, ACLED features the event type "Violence Against Civilians". However, to classify most of the concerned events, the annotator needs to know if the target is a civilian or not. Unfortunately, the dataset does not always contain this information, except if explicitly written in the event description. Another frequently observed error is caused by blurry definition of event types. ACLED, differentiates between "Riots" and "Protests" which often have nearly identical event descriptions.

6 Human-Computer Codebook Design

To make use of PR-ENT, domain experts need to design a codebook (i.e. a mapping), between event types and entailed answer candidates. Creating this mapping is non-trivial as there exists a trade-off between interpretability and accuracy. In essence, a codebook is interpretable when the answer candidates are representative of the corresponding event type. A bad codebook contains a large number of non-readable entailed answer candidates. A codebook is accurate when a few answer candidates are sufficient to allow for a clear differentiation of the event types. To that end, we propose an interactive codebook design tool[6] that helps designing templates and answer candidates by presenting accuracy metrics. The assessment of interpretability is left to the human domain experts.

Codebook Design. Our codebook is a mapping between event types and entailed answer candidates. For example, an event can be classified as "kidnapping" if any of the following templates is

[6] https://huggingface.co/spaces/clef/PRENT-Codebook

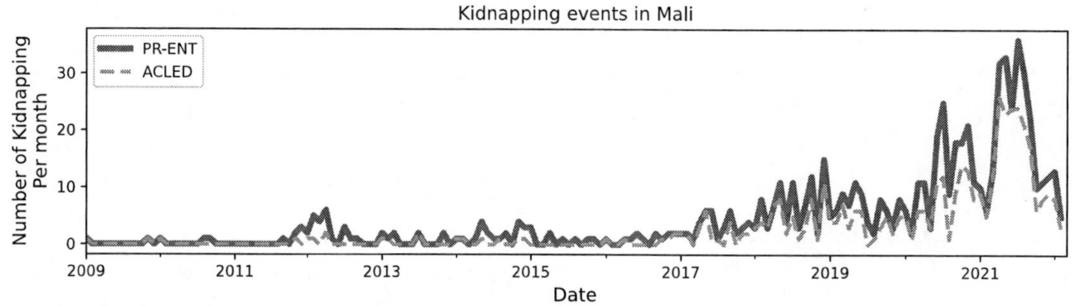

Figure 6: Time series of the number of kidnapping events per month in Mali between 2009-2021. The dashed line corresponds to all kidnapping events coded by ACLED annotators. The blue line corresponds to all kidnapping events coded by PR-ENT. We find that the positions of the time series spikes between PR-ENT and ACLED's coding align well. However, the spikes in the PR-ENT time series are higher indicating that PR-ENT detects more events. This may be due to more granular event coding or the advantage of not being limited to only one event type per event description.

entailed: "This event involves [kidnapping]." OR "This event involves [abduction].". A codebook example is shown in Tab. 7 in the appendix.

We assume two things: first, the availability of a dataset which contains event descriptions that need to be labeled. Second, the domain experts should have decided upon event types of their liking (e.g. kidnapping, killings,...). Now, the first step is to come up with an initial set of templates and entailed answer candidates. For each event type, the domain expert is asked to draft a canonical event description. For example: the event type "kidnapping" could be exemplified by "Two men were kidnapped by rebels.". Then using PR-ENT, the domain expert is presented a list of answer candidates (e.g. "This event involves [kidnapping].", "This event involves [rebels]."...).

As a second step, domain experts select some of the entailed answer candidates provided by the model. If no entailed answer candidate is informative to classify the event, it is possible to group multiple entailed answer candidates with an AND condition. For example, "Riot" event types can be coded with the two following templates: "This event involves [protest]." AND "This event involves [violence].". The tool also offers the possibility of excluding certain answer candidates.

On-the-Go Validation. Validating the interpretability of the codebook and the answer candidates is a subjective task that we leave to the domain experts. The coding tools offers however guidance for the validation of accuracy, despite not having access to ground truth event type labels. Using the current state of the codebook and PR-ENT, randomly selected events are automatically coded into event types. Domain experts can then accept or reject the event type suggestions provided by the model. This creates a labeled dataset "on the go", which allows computing a per-class accuracy score. Repeated rounds of validation allow for a human-in-the-loop fine-tuning of the codebook by adding or removing more entailed answer candidates.

Codebook Use. The tool offers interoperability by enabling the download of the codebook and the labeled dataset in standard JSON format. The former can then be used to code a full dataset of event descriptions into event types. The codebook can still be modified if more event types are required.

7 Discussion

Is this few-shot, unsupervised tagging? While we have evaluated accuracy, efficiency and flexibility, it is up for discussion and definition whether our approach should be considered few-shot, unsupervised or tagging-based. In some cases, the language model copies tokens verbatim from the input, which could be seen as a form of "event tagging". In other cases, the answer candidates are abstract tokens outperforming purely tagging-based approaches. In cases where the answer candidates map directly to an event type without an additional shallow classifier §4.2, our approach may be considered unsupervised and zero-shot. On the contrary, the template is designed in an iterative trial and error fashion. Thus, it is tuned to observed data instances which arguably violates the zero-shot setting and should be framed few-shot instead.

Entailment-Only Approach. The presented approach PR-ENT relies on textual entailment to select entailed answer candidates from prompts as motivated in §3.2. However, textual entailment could have been considered for classification by itself (Wang et al., 2021; Barker et al., 2021). In this setting: a predefined set of hypotheses is created for each event type and is tested against each event description. However, this reduces flexibility as we need to define a broad set of hypotheses in advance. Our prompting-based approach relies on large language models which do not require labeled training data for training. As a consequence, they are more frequently updated and trained on larger amounts of data.

Extensions and Applications. Our approach can be used to filter and search events in a dataset of full-text event descriptions. An example of this use case is described in §4.2 where we classify lethal and non-lethal events in an unsupervised way via the "killed" token. Promising extension are the coding of source and target actors in addition to event types as presented in App. B.1 as well as the extraction of victim counts (Zhong et al., 2023).

8 Related Work

Similar to our prompting-based approach, existing work evaluates off-the-shelf QA (Halterman et al., 2021) and NLI (Barker et al., 2021) models for event coding. The prompting approach shares similarities with Shin et al. (2021), who build a semantic parser to map natural text to canonical utterances. Their training set is constructed by prompting a language model in a human-in-the-loop fashion. Sainz et al. (2021) uses NLI to extract relationship between two given entities based on a predefined hypothesis template. Schick et al. (2020) present an approach to identify words that can serve as high-accuracy labels for text classification. However, they are not focusing on interpretability and a particular application domain such as political event coding. There also exist methods for automating prompt generation and selective incorporation of examples in the prompt (Shin et al., 2020; Gao et al., 2021). Existing work in prompt-based classification focuses on sentiment, topic or intent (Yin et al., 2019; Liu et al., 2021; Schick and Schütze, 2021).

Within the field of event coding, we distinguish work on event detection, event type ontologies, and automated event coding tools. Our work falls into the latter two. The World Event/Interaction Survey (WEIS) project (McClelland, 1984) was pioneering in event data collection and event ontology design. The WEIS successor CAMEO (Schrodt, 2012) is one of the most popular event ontologies until today and used by ICEWS (Boschee et al., 2015) and NAVCO (Lewis et al., 2016) among others. VRA-Reader (King and Lowe, 2003) is among the first to automatize event coding based on matching string patterns. Its successors BBN ACCENT (Boschee et al., 2015), Tabari and Petrarch2 (Norris et al., 2017) rely on lambda calculus-based semantic parsing. Recent event coding systems rely on supervised machine learning (Hürriyetoğlu, 2021; Stoehr et al., 2021, 2022, 2023), word embedding-(Kutuzov et al., 2017; Piskorski and Jacquet, 2020) and transformer-based models (Olsson et al., 2020; Re et al., 2021; Hu et al., 2022; Skorupa Parolin et al., 2022).

9 Conclusion

We proposed a method to select answer candidates from prompts using textual entailment. This combined usage of state-of-the-art tools is motivated by a real-world use case that benefits humanitarian aid efforts with scarce resources.

https://github.com/Clement-Lef/pr-ent

Acknowledgments

This work was funded by the ETH4D Humanitarian Action Challenge and grew out of a collaboration with Roberto Castello, Silvia Quarteroni, Daniel Gatica-Perez and Sandro Saitta. We would like to thank Fiona Terry, Francesca Grandi and Chiara Debenedetti from the International Committee of the Red Cross (ICRC) for feedback and discussions that motivated this research project. Niklas Stoehr is supported by a scholarship from the Swiss Data Science Center (SDSC).

Limitations

We explore potential failure modes and the impact of bias in pre-trained (cloze) language models in §5. Erroneous event coding can be further mitigated through incorporation of confidence score. In §7, we discuss definitional caveats and model limitations. We make our code and interactive dashboard available for replication and scrutiny by the scientific community. We provide hyperparameter settings, training times and details on the computing infrastructure in the appendix (App. A). Since we are only considering off-the-shelf models, mostly without further fine-tuning, our experiments can be reproduced with limited computing resources. Our experiments are limited to English language, but can be extended by considering models pre-trained on other language data.

Impact Statement

As explained in §1, our approach is aimed at helping low-resource organizations to analyze large amounts of text data efficiently. We do not foresee risk of misuse beyond the risks already introduced by conventional event coding pipelines. However, we would like to emphasize that the intended use of our approach is to gain additional, empirical insights for research and monitoring purposes, rather than for completely automatized decision-making. Application cases such as filtering event datasets are described in §7 and App. B.1 .

References

Ken Barker, Parul Awasthy, Jian Ni, and Radu Florian. 2021. IBM MNLP IE at CASE 2021 Task 2: NLI Reranking for Zero-Shot Text Classification. In *Proceedings of the 4th Workshop on Challenges and Applications of Automated Extraction of Socio-political Events from Text (CASE 2021)*, pages 193–202, Online. Association for Computational Linguistics.

Elizabeth Boschee, Jennifer Lautenschlager, Sean O'Brien, Steve Shellman, James Starz, and Michael Ward. 2015. ICEWS Coded Event Data.

Samuel R. Bowman, Gabor Angeli, Christopher Potts, and Christopher D. Manning. 2015. A large annotated corpus for learning natural language inference. In *Proceedings of the 2015 Conference on Empirical Methods in Natural Language Processing*, pages 632–642.

Yaroslav Fyodorov, Yoad Winter, and Nissim Francez. 2000. A Natural Logic Inference System.

Tianyu Gao, Adam Fisch, and Danqi Chen. 2021. Making Pre-trained Language Models Better Few-shot Learners. In *Proceedings of the 59th Annual Meeting of the Association for Computational Linguistics*, pages 3816–3830.

Joshua Goldstein. 1992. A conflict-cooperation scale for WEIS events data. *The Journal of Conflict Resolution*, 36(2):369–385.

Andrew Halterman, Katherine Keith, Sheikh Sarwar, and Brendan O'Connor. 2021. Corpus-Level Evaluation for Event QA: The IndiaPoliceEvents Corpus Covering the 2002 Gujarat Violence. In *Findings of the Association for Computational Linguistics: ACL-IJCNLP*, pages 4240–4253, Online.

Luheng He, Mike Lewis, and Luke Zettlemoyer. 2015. Question-Answer Driven Semantic Role Labeling: Using Natural Language to Annotate Natural Language. In *Proceedings of the 2015 Conference on Empirical Methods in Natural Language Processing*, pages 643–653.

Yibo Hu, MohammadSaleh Hosseini, Erick Skorupa Parolin, Javier Osorio, Latifur Khan, Patrick T. Brandt, and Vito J. D'Orazio. 2022. ConfliBERT: A pre-trained language model for political conflict and violence. In *Proceedings of the 2022 Conference of the North American Chapter of the Association for Computational Linguistics*.

Ali Hürriyetoğlu, editor. 2021. *Proceedings of the 4th Workshop on Challenges and Applications of Automated Extraction of Socio-political Events from Text (CASE 2021)*. Association for Computational Linguistics.

Gary King and Will Lowe. 2003. An automated information extraction tool for international conflict data with performance as good as human coders: A rare events evaluation design. *International Organization*, 57(3):617–642.

Andrey Kutuzov, Erik Velldal, and Lilja Øvrelid. 2017. Tracing armed conflicts with diachronic word embedding models. In *Proceedings of the Events and Stories in the News Workshop*, pages 31–36.

Gary LaFree and Laura Dugan. 2007. Introducing the Global Terrorism Database. *Terrorism and Political Violence*, 19(2):181–204. Publisher: Routledge.

Raphael Lepuschitz and Niklas Stoehr. 2021. SeismographAPI: Visualising temporal-spatial crisis data. *KDD Workshop on Data-Driven Humanitarian Mapping*, 2107.12443(arXiv).

Orion A. Lewis, Erica Chenoweth, and Jonathan Pinckney. 2016. Nonviolent and violent campaigns and outcomes 3.0: Effects of tactical choices on strategic outcomes codebook.

Pengfei Liu, Weizhe Yuan, Jinlan Fu, Zhengbao Jiang, Hiroaki Hayashi, and Graham Neubig. 2021. Pretrain, Prompt, and Predict: A Systematic Survey of Prompting Methods in Natural Language Processing. *arXiv*, 2107.13586.

Yinhan Liu, Myle Ott, Naman Goyal, Jingfei Du, Mandar Joshi, Danqi Chen, Omer Levy, Mike Lewis, Luke Zettlemoyer, and Veselin Stoyanov. 2019. RoBERTa: A Robustly Optimized BERT Pretraining Approach. *arXiv*, 1907.11692.

Charles McClelland. 1984. World event/interaction survey (WEIS) project, 1966-1978: Archival version.

Clayton Norris, Philip Schrodt, and John Beieler. 2017. Petrarch2: Another event coding program. *The Journal of Open Source Software*, 2.

Fredrik Olsson, Magnus Sahlgren, Fehmi ben Abdesslem, Ariel Ekgren, and Kristine Eck. 2020. Text Categorization for Conflict Event Annotation. In *Proceedings of the Workshop on Automated Extraction of Socio-political Events from News 2020*.

Jeffrey Pennington, Richard Socher, and Christopher Manning. 2014. Glove: Global vectors for word representation. In *Proceedings of the 2014 Conference on Empirical Methods in Natural Language Processing*, pages 1532–1543.

Jakub Piskorski and Guillaume Jacquet. 2020. TF-IDF Character N-grams versus Word Embedding-based Models for Fine-grained Event Classification: A Preliminary Study. In *Proceedings of the Workshop on Automated Extraction of Socio-political Events from News 2020*.

Pranav Rajpurkar, Jian Zhang, Konstantin Lopyrev, and Percy Liang. 2016. SQuAD: 100,000+ Questions for Machine Comprehension of Text. In *Proceedings of the 2016 Conference on Empirical Methods in Natural Language Processing*, pages 2383–2392.

Clionadh Raleigh, Andrew Linke, Håvard Hegre, and Joakim Karlsen. 2010. Introducing ACLED-Armed Conflict Location and Event Data. *Journal of Peace Research*, 47(5):651–660.

Francesco Re, Daniel Vegh, Dennis Atzenhofer, and Niklas Stoehr. 2021. Team "DaDeFrNi" at CASE 2021 Task 1: Document and sentence classification for protest event detection. In *Challenges and Applications of Automated Extraction of Socio-political Events from Text*, pages 171–178.

Oscar Sainz, Oier Lopez de Lacalle, Gorka Labaka, Ander Barrena, and Eneko Agirre. 2021. Label verbalization and entailment for effective zero- and few-shot relation extraction. *CoRR*, abs/2109.03659.

Victor Sanh, Lysandre Debut, Julien Chaumond, and Thomas Wolf. 2020. DistilBERT, a distilled version of BERT: smaller, faster, cheaper and lighter. *arXiv*, 1910.01108.

Timo Schick, Helmut Schmid, and Hinrich Schütze. 2020. Automatically Identifying Words That Can Serve as Labels for Few-Shot Text Classification. In *Proceedings of the 28th International Conference on Computational Linguistics*, pages 5569–5578.

Timo Schick and Hinrich Schütze. 2021. Exploiting Cloze-Questions for Few-Shot Text Classification and Natural Language Inference. In *Proceedings of the 16th Conference of the European Chapter of the Association for Computational Linguistics*.

Philip Schrodt. 2012. CAMEO: Conflict and mediation event observations event and actor codebook. *Parus Analytics*.

Richard Shin, Christopher Lin, Sam Thomson, Charles Chen, Subhro Roy, Emmanouil Antonios Platanios, Adam Pauls, Dan Klein, Jason Eisner, and Benjamin Van Durme. 2021. Constrained Language Models Yield Few-Shot Semantic Parsers. In *Proceedings of the 2021 Conference on Empirical Methods in Natural Language Processing*.

Taylor Shin, Yasaman Razeghi, Robert L. Logan IV, Eric Wallace, and Sameer Singh. 2020. AutoPrompt: Eliciting Knowledge from Language Models with Automatically Generated Prompts. In *Proceedings of the 2020 Conference on Empirical Methods in Natural Language Processing (EMNLP)*, pages 4222–4235.

Erick Skorupa Parolin, MohammadSaleh Hosseini, Yibo Hu, Latifur Khan, Patrick T. Brandt, Javier Osorio, and Vito D'Orazio. 2022. Multi-CoPED: A Multilingual Multi-Task Approach for Coding Political Event Data on Conflict and Mediation Domain. In *Proceedings of the 2022 AAAI/ACM Conference on AI, Ethics, and Society*, pages 700–711, Oxford United Kingdom. ACM.

Niklas Stoehr, Lucas Torroba Hennigen, Samin Ahbab, Robert West, and Ryan Cotterell. 2021. Classifying dyads for militarized conflict analysis. In *Proceedings of the 2021 Conference on Empirical Methods in Natural Language Processing (EMNLP)*.

Niklas Stoehr, Lucas Torroba Hennigen, Josef Valvoda, Robert West, Ryan Cotterell, and Aaron Schein. 2022. An ordinal latent variable model of conflict intensity. In *arXiv*, volume 2210.03971.

Niklas Stoehr, Benjamin J. Radford, Ryan Cotterell, and Aaron Schein. 2023. The Ordered Matrix Dirichlet for state-space models. In *AISTATS*.

Umair ul Hassan, Sean O'Riain, and Edward Curry. 2013. SLUA: Towards Semantic Linking of Users with Actions in Crowdsourcing. In *CEUR Workshop Proceedings*, volume 1030.

Sinong Wang, Han Fang, Madian Khabsa, Hanzi Mao, and Hao Ma. 2021. Entailment as Few-Shot Learner. *CoRR*, abs/2104.14690. ArXiv: 2104.14690.

Wenpeng Yin, Jamaal Hay, and Dan Roth. 2019. Benchmarking Zero-shot Text Classification: Datasets, Evaluation and Entailment Approach. In *Proceedings of the 2019 Conference on Empirical Methods in Natural Language Processing and the 9th International Joint Conference on Natural Language Processing (EMNLP-IJCNLP)*, pages 3912–3921, Hong Kong, China. Association for Computational Linguistics.

Mian Zhong, Shehzaad Dhuliawala, and Niklas Stoehr. 2023. Extracting victim counts from text. In *European Chapter of the ACL (EACL)*.

A Reproducibility Criteria

A.1 Experimental Results

1. A clear description of the mathematical setting, algorithm, and/or model
   - See Section §3
2. Submission of a zip file containing source code, with specification of all dependencies, including external libraries, or a link to such resources (while still anonymized)
   - Provided in the submission
3. Description of computing infrastructure used
   - PR-ENT inference: Dell Latitude 7490 laptop - Intel(R) Core(TM) i7-8650U CPU @ 1.90GHz / 16 GB RAM
   - DistilBERT finetuning: Macbook Pro M1 Max - M1 Max / 32 GB RAM
   - Dashboard: 8 CPU Cores / 16 GB RAM
4. The average runtime for each model or algorithm (e.g., training, inference, etc.), or estimated energy cost
   - Training:
     - No training done for PR-ENT
     - For comparison purposes, a DistilBERT model was fine-tuned on 3000 samples. It took several minutes on a laptop.
   - Inference:
     - PR-ENT: 1-10secs per text depending on text length on a laptop
5. Number of parameters in each model:
   - DistilBERT-base-uncased (https://huggingface.co/distilbert-base-uncased): 65M
   - RoBERTa-large-mnli (https://huggingface.co/roberta-large-mnli): 125M
   - RoBERTA-large-squad2 (https://huggingface.co/deepset/roberta-large-squad2): 125M
   - PR-ENT: Top K, Entailment Threshold
6. Corresponding validation performance for each reported test result
   - Not applicable
7. Explanation of evaluation metrics used, with links to code
   - F1 Score, Scikit-learn
   - Precision, Scikit-learn
   - Recall, Scikit-learn
   - Accuracy, Scikit-learn
   - Jensen Shannon Distance, Scipy

A.2 Hyperparameter Search

Not applicable

A.3 Datasets

1. Relevant details such as languages, and number of examples and label distributions
   - ACLED: See section §2
   - GTD: See section §2
2. Details of train/validation/test splits
   - ACLED: 3000 train sample / 1000 test sample
   - GTD: 100 train sample / 1000 test sample
3. Explanation of any data that were excluded, and all pre-processing steps
   - See section §2
4. A zip file containing data or link to a downloadable version of the data
   - ACLED: Data is not open source. We provide a json file containing the event ID used in train and test set.
   - GTD: Data is available on GTD Website : We provide a json file containing the event ID used in train and test set
   - Provided in the submission
5. For new data collected, a complete description of the data collection process, such as instructions to annotators and methods for quality control.
   - Not applicable

B Additional Material

B.1 Actor and Target Coding.

Until now, we studied how to code event types, which can be seen as actions or predicates of an event. We propose an extension to extract the actor and target of an event using question answering models similar to Halterman et al. (2021). In He et al. (2015), questions are constructed around a known action performed in an event. Given the example "Military injured two civilians.", PR-ENT yields "injured" as an action. Using this action, we can construct the questions "Who was injured?" and "Who injured people?" which are then fed to a QA model RoBERTa-base-squad2 (Rajpurkar et al., 2016). We present examples of extracted "who-did-what-to-whom" patterns in Tab. 6. Actor-target coding is even harder to evaluate, as there can be multiple actions / targets / actors in an event description and the abstract mapping between manually annotated entity types (e.g. civilians) and verbatim mentions (e.g. demonstrators) is not known.

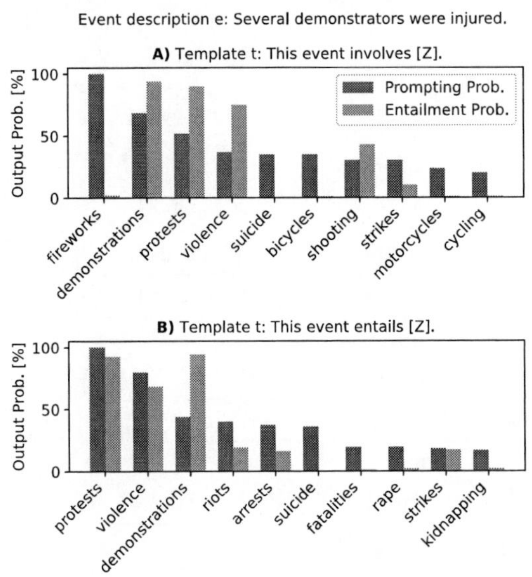

Figure 7: Given the event description *"Several demonstrators were injured."*, and the two similar templates **(A)** and **(B)**, we get drastically different answer candidates as shown by the top 10 outputs of the prompt model (blue bar). However, in both cases we obtain the same 3 answer candidates if they are filtered through an additional entailment step (orange bar).

Event Description + Extracted Actor-Target	Action
Arrests: **[WHO (31%): [LOC] police]** captured **[WHOM (90%): [NAME]]**, a senior [ORG] in [LOC]	arrested
On 3 January 2020, **[WHO (17%): [LOC] Armed Forces]** regained [LOC], [LOC], [LOC], [LOC] and [LOC] from [ORG]. In the operations 6 [ORG] fighters were arrested and **[WHOM (67%): 461 kidnapped civilians]** were rescued.	rescued
On 12 March 2020, **[WHO (40%): police and military intelligence officers]** raided the home of retired **[WHOM (15%, 6%): Lt. Gen [NAME]]**. The candidate was arrested and charged with treason in relation to remarks he made during a [WHO (29%): TV] interview; his staff of 18, as well as the MP for [ORG] as well as his son have all been arrested.	**arrested**; interviewed

Table 6: Actor-target coding based on our pipeline augmented with an additional extractive question-answering (QA) model. The first example represents a clear "who-did-what-to-whom" pattern. In the second example, actor and target are separated into two sentences. Finally, the third example shows an event with two *ARG0-V-ARG1* patterns (bolded and underlined). The confidence of the QA model is displayed for each answer.

Event Type	Template	Entailed Answer Candidate
Arrest	People were $[Z]$.	arrested AND NOT kidnapped
Killing	This event involves $[Z]$.	killing
	People were $[Z]$.	killed
Looting	This event involves $[Z]$.	looting OR theft OR robbery
Sexual Violence	This event involves $[Z]$.	rape
	People were $[Z]$.	abused OR raped
Kidnapping	This event involves $[Z]$.	kidnapping
	People were $[Z]$.	kidnapped OR abducted
Protest	This event involves $[Z]$.	protest OR demonstration
	People were $[Z]$.	protesting

Table 7: Example of an event ontology designed by means of our approach of entailment-based prompt selection PR-ENT. The final ontology is defined in terms of templates and expected entailed answer candidates. We use the event type "Killing" versus all others to classify "lethal" versus "non-lethal" events in Tab. 3. It's also used to compute results of Fig. 6 and Fig. 10.

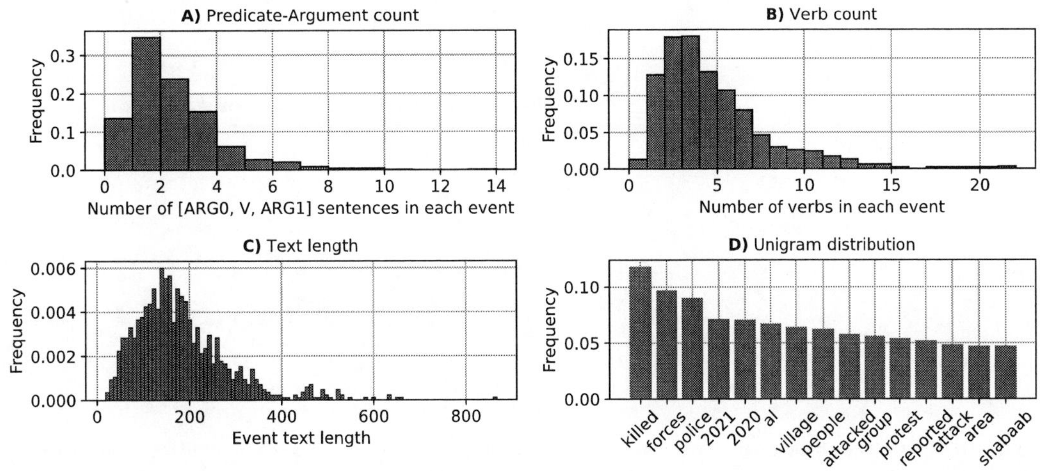

Figure 8: Statistics over a sample of 1000 ACLED event descriptions; **(A)** encountering many predicate-argument structures per event description can be an indication of difficult event coding; **(B)** number of verbs (actions) per event description; **(C)** length distribution of event descriptions; **(D)** unigram distribution over dataset.

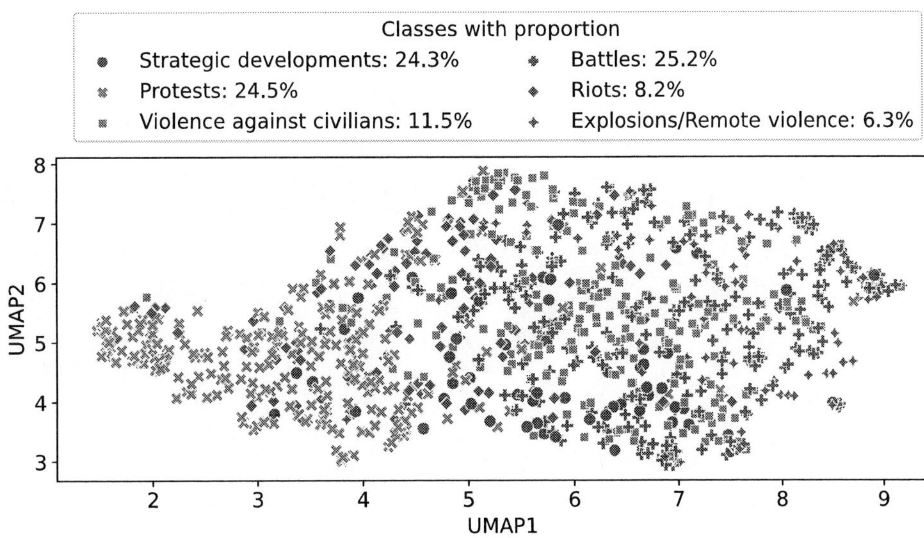

Figure 9: Event type distribution as visualized using UMAP over GloVe embeddings of the event descriptions. While some event types are easily distinguishable from each other (e.g. *Protests* and *Battles*), others are harder to tell apart (e.g. *Protests* and *Riots*). We also show the proportion of each event type in the legend.

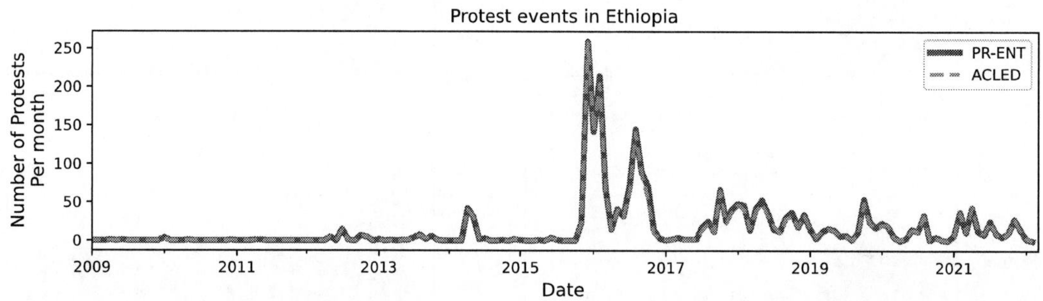

Figure 10: Time series of the number of protest events per month in Ethiopia between 2009-2021. The dashed line corresponds to all protest events coded by ACLED annotators. The blue line corresponds to all protest events coded by PR-ENT. Despite PR-ENT codings being machine-automated, they are very similar to ACLED's codings. Both clearly detect the high intensity violence periods in 2016.

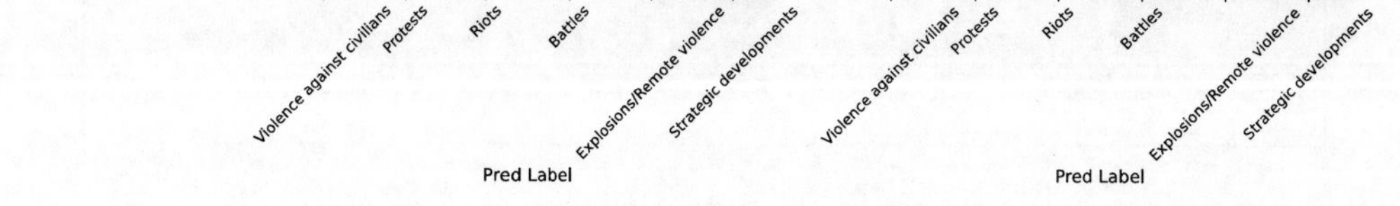

Figure 11: Confusion matrices of DistilBERT and PR-ENT + LR on the test set.

Hierarchical Representations in Dense Passage Retrieval for Question-Answering

Philipp Ennen, Federica Freddi, Chyi-Jiunn Lin, Po-Nien Kung
RenChu Wang, Chien-Yi Yang, Da-Shan Shiu, Alberto Bernacchia
MediaTek Research
{philipp.ennen, alberto.bernacchia}@mtkresearch.com

Abstract

An approach to improve question-answering performance is to retrieve accompanying information that contains factual evidence matching the question. These retrieved documents are then fed into a reader that generates an answer. A commonly applied retriever is dense passage retrieval. In this retriever, the output of a transformer neural network is used to query a knowledge database for matching documents. Inspired by the observation that different layers of a transformer network provide rich representations with different levels of abstraction, we hypothesize that useful queries can be generated not only at the output layer, but at every layer of a transformer network, and that the hidden representations of different layers may combine to improve the fetched documents for reader performance. Our novel approach integrates retrieval into each layer of a transformer network, exploiting the hierarchical representations of the input question. We show that our technique outperforms prior work on downstream tasks such as question answering, demonstrating the effectiveness of our approach.

When did Harvard become an Ivy League school?	
FetcHR:	*Harvard*: 300, *Ivy League*: 109
DPR:	*Harvard*: 341, *Ivy League*: 66
Who overthrew the Mongols and established the Ming Dynasty?	
FetcHR:	*Mongols*: 108, *Ming*: 112
DPR:	*Mongols*: 108, *Ming*: 87
When did the Soviet Union first gain control of parts of Poland and the Baltic Republics?	
FetcHR:	*Soviet Union*: 139, *Poland*: 93 , *Baltic Republics*: 7
DPR:	*Soviet Union*: 133, *Poland*: 214, *Baltic Republics*: 2

Figure 1: We present the occurrences of word features inside the document collection as retrieved by either DPR or FetcHR. The feature from the question with the lowest occurrence is the critical feature for QA tasks. Our retriever FetcHR outperforms DPR on critical word features in the question (underlined). Our work shows that this improved document collection increases the reader performance by up to 1.9 EM score on Natural Question and 2.1 EM score on WebQuestion.

1 Introduction

In open book question answering, the answer to a given question needs to be generated from a large pool of passages. Typically, this problem is tackled in two stages. Given a question, a retriever collects a set of top-k passages from the passages memory. Then, a reader generates the answer from the retrieved documents. In this setting, dense passage retrieval (DPR) is a commonly used retriever (Karpukhin et al., 2020). Therein, each passage in a document collection is represented as a vector in a high-dimensional space. These vectors are then used to compute similarity scores between passages. The most similar passages are then retrieved and used as input to a machine learning model.

However, we observe that current open-book QA systems do not adequately exploit the correlations between passages in the retrieved document collection. Typically, questions contain several word features that need to be represented in the retrieved document collection, i.e. questions in Figure 1. In order to answer such questions, the reader needs to reason about multiple word features of the question simultaneously. However, we found that many questions have a critical feature that is underrepresented in the retrieved documents (i.e. Ivy League, Ming, Baltic Republic). In order to improve the QA performance, we propose to increase the occurrence on these critical features.

Typically, the retrieved document collection matches the highest abstraction level of an input question. We hypothesize that a document collection addressing different, hierarchical abstraction levels of an input question may improve on the critical features. With these documents, the reader improves the performance on question-answering benchmarks.

We present a novel retriever architecture and training procedure to test this hypothesis (Figure

Proceedings of the Sixth Fact Extraction and VERification Workshop (FEVER), pages 17–28
May 5, 2023 ©2023 Association for Computational Linguistics

2). Our architecture extends BERT (Devlin et al., 2019) with a neural retrieval network producing queries not only at its output layer but also at intermediate layers. This is inspired by the observation that different layers provide different level of abstraction (Rogers et al., 2020) that can be all used for downstream tasks (Evci et al., 2022). Under this setup, the retrievable documents embody a non-parametric knowledge of the transformer (Guu et al., 2020). With a separate reader function, an answer is inferred from the documents retrieved by the hierarchical retrievers (see section 3 for details of the model).

Our main contributions are:

- We introduce FetcHR, a document fetcher based on hierarchical retrieval. We equip transformer layers with a neural retrieval network allowing hidden representations to contribute to the retrieval query.
- We show that retrieval performance of all layers combined is higher than any of the individual layers, in most of our experiments. This allows improving performance of previous models, which considered retrieval from single layers only.
- When using a reader to generate the answer to the input question, we show that documents retrieved by FetcHR obtain the highest performance in all experiments, and advance the state-of-the-art on the Natural Question and WebQuestion datasets.
- All results are obtained by training only the retrieval networks. This avoids any modification of the underlying language model, making it feasible to customize a large pretrained language model with moderate training resources.

2 Related Work

Retrieval Question-answering tasks are usually tackled introducing retrieval components in order to efficiently select a subset of relevant documents (Voorhees et al., 1999). In the past, Q&A tasks would be generally attempted using sparse vector space models such as BM25 and TF-IDF (Chen et al., 2017; Yang et al., 2019; Nie et al., 2019; Wolfson et al., 2020; Min et al., 2019). In the past few years, these were replaced by transformer-based models mapping a model input to a dense vector representation. There are mainly two approaches of neural network-based retrievers based on single or multiple embedding vectors (Singh et al., 2021). Dual encoders belong to the single embedding approaches. Such retrievers use one encoder for the documents and another one for the query (Yih et al., 2011; Lee et al., 2019). Dense Passage Retrieval (DPR) (Karpukhin et al., 2020) uses two BERT-style models to learn a similarity metric between document and query. In case of multi-vector retrievers instead, multiple embeddings are generated for each document, such as in (Khattab and Zaharia, 2020; Zhang et al., 2022; Luan et al., 2021). However this approach is computationally limiting in large-scale retrieval since it requires to retrieve in many search spaces (up to the document token length) leading to increased memory needs and search time. Instead we propose to perform retrieval in each layer of a BERT-based transformer network limiting the retrieval runs to 12. This approach borrows ideas from early work in information retrieval on multi-layer matching (Nie et al., 2018a,b), however retrieval is performed based on an aggregated score over all layers. Instead, our approach performs retrieval in each layer, while using a more modern transformer architecture, scales to large-scale retrieval and is evaluated on end-to-end QA.

Training of Dual Encoders Past work has shown (Qu et al., 2021; Guu et al., 2020; Lewis et al., 2020; Singh et al., 2021) that the performance of dual encoders can be improved by (i) carefully selecting negative documents for the contrastive loss and (ii) by an end-to-end training with a reader function. Cross-batch negatives, denoised hard negatives and data augmentation are options mentioned in (Qu et al., 2021) for negative documents. End-to-end training approaches tune the retrieval function to match the distribution of data for the reader (Lewis et al., 2020; Guu et al., 2020; Singh et al., 2021). These approaches are orthogonal to our work and might be considered as an extension for future work.

3 FetcHR Model

3.1 Retrieval Score

The purpose of a retrieval system is to choose a selection of documents from a collection of documents (referred to as the "Document Memory") that contains pertinent information to answer a given

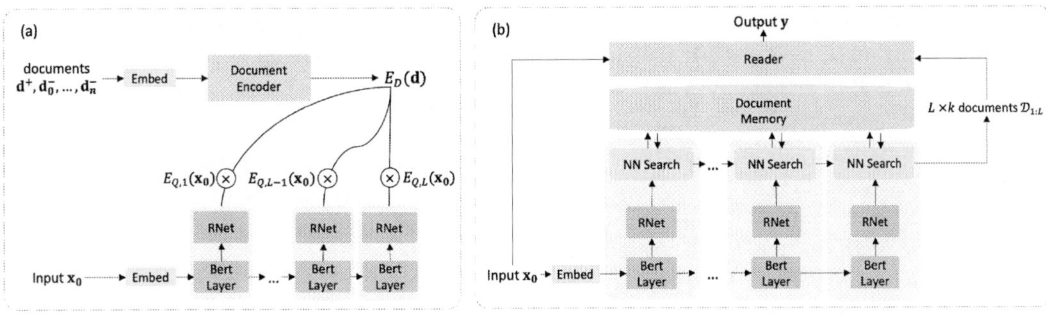

Figure 2: FetcHR is a stack of BERT layers with an additional Retrieval Network (RNet) at each layer. (**a**) Training: The inner product between the encoded input question at each layer $E_{Q,\ell}(\mathbf{x}_0)$ and the encoded document $E_D(\mathbf{d})$ is maximised for positive documents $\mathbf{d}^+$ and minimized for negative documents $\mathbf{d}^-$, using a contrastive loss. (**b**) Inference: Using nearest neighbour search, FetcHR retrieves k documents per layer from the document memory, for a total $L \times k$ documents. The reader outputs the answer $\mathbf{y}$ given the hierarchy of retrieved documents combined with the model input $\mathbf{x}_0$

tokenized input question $\mathbf{x}_0$. Our novel retrieval system *FetcHR* gathers documents for different hierarchical representations of the model input. For this, we employ a multi-layer encoder architecture. Each layer ℓ has its own encoder function $E_{Q,\ell}$, which is used to query the document memory. This allows us to define a retrieval score as the inner product between the vector pairs $E_{Q,\ell}$ and E_D for all layers. Given a question $\mathbf{x}_0$ and document $\mathbf{d}$, the retrieval score for layer ℓ can be computed via the inner product between the vector pairs $E_{Q,\ell}$ and E_D

$$\text{score}_\ell = E_{Q,\ell}(\mathbf{x}_0; \boldsymbol{\theta}_{1:\ell}, \boldsymbol{\phi}_\ell) \cdot E_D(\mathbf{d}; \boldsymbol{\omega}) \quad (1)$$

The parameters $\boldsymbol{\theta}_{1:\ell}$ are shared by the first ℓ layers, while $\boldsymbol{\phi}_\ell$ corresponds to the parameters specific to layer ℓ, and $\boldsymbol{\omega}$ is the parameter vector of the document encoder. Consequently, the retrieval score in layer ℓ depends on a layer-specific question encoder $E_{Q,\ell}$ and a single, shared document encoder E_D for all layers.

3.2 Contrastive Training

During training, we present data points to the model. Each one is a tuple of an input question $\mathbf{x}_0$, a positive document $\mathbf{d}^+$ containing the correct answer to the question and n negative (randomly chosen) documents $\mathbf{d}_1^-, ..., \mathbf{d}_n^-$. The training goal is to improve the retrieval score of all layers at the same time. Following (Karpukhin et al., 2020), we adopt the contrastive loss function which, for a single data point $\{\mathbf{x}_0, \mathbf{d}^+, \mathbf{d}_1^-, ..., \mathbf{d}_n^-\}$, is equal to

$$\mathcal{L}(\boldsymbol{\phi}, \boldsymbol{\theta}, \boldsymbol{\omega}) =$$
$$\frac{1}{L}\sum_{\ell=1}^{L} -\log \frac{e^{\text{score}_\ell(\mathbf{x}_0,\mathbf{d}^+)}}{e^{\text{score}_\ell(\mathbf{x}_0,\mathbf{d}^+)} + \sum_{i=1}^{n} e^{\text{score}_\ell(\mathbf{x}_0,\mathbf{d}_i^-)}}$$

This loss is minimized by adjusting the parameters $\boldsymbol{\phi}$ while holding $\boldsymbol{\theta}$ and $\boldsymbol{\omega}$ constant to the pre-trained values from (Karpukhin et al., 2020). The loss is calculated and averaged over a batch of data points at each iteration (see Section 4.2 for details).

3.3 Multi-layer encoder

FetcHR is build on top of BERT transformer layers (Devlin et al., 2019). We use a stack of these BERT layers and define for each layer ℓ a retrieval network *RNet* to generate single query vectors $\mathbf{q}_\ell = E_{Q,\ell}(\mathbf{x})$. Formally, the encoder function $E_{Q,\ell}$ is obtained according to

$$\mathbf{x}_\ell = \textit{BertLayer}(\mathbf{x}_{\ell-1}, \boldsymbol{\theta}_\ell) \qquad \text{for } \ell = 1, \ldots, L$$
$$E_{Q,\ell} = \textit{RNet}(\mathbf{x}_\ell; \boldsymbol{\phi}_\ell) \quad (2)$$

where the parameters $\boldsymbol{\phi}_\ell$ corresponds to the retrieval network and $\boldsymbol{\theta}_\ell$ to BERT layer ℓ. Note that the encoder function $E_{Q,\ell}$ depends on the input question $\mathbf{x}_0$ and the parameters $\boldsymbol{\theta}_{1:\ell}$ of all upstream BERT layers through $\mathbf{x}_\ell$.

The output of the retrieval network *RNet* is the embedding at the CLS position of the output of a stack of two transformer layers. Each layer is a BERT transformer layer, with the skip connection placed outside of the layer normalization:

$$\textit{LayerNorm}(\mathbf{W}_2(\sigma_1(\mathbf{W}_1(\textit{AttnLayer}(\cdot)))) + \textit{AttnLayer}(\cdot) \quad (3)$$

where W and σ are the weights and activation function, respectively, of a two-layer MLP as in standard self-attention. Placing the skip connection outside of layer normalization is advantageous when *BertLayer* is initialized with pre-trained weights such that $\mathbf{x}_\ell$ already captures a meaningful abstraction of the input question. In all of our experiments, we use a combination of the *BertLayer* and the *RNet*, which we refer to as the *FetcHR layer*. We use $L = 12$ layers in total. All of the embeddings are 768-dimensional, as in the original BERT model. For the document encoder $E_D(\mathbf{d}; \boldsymbol{\omega})$, we use a BERT model in base configuration. The pre-trained parameters $\boldsymbol{\omega}$ come from (Karpukhin et al., 2020).

3.4 Inference

After training, retrieval on test data is implemented by matching the FetcHR encodings of each layer with document encodings in the document memory. For each layer ℓ, a set $\mathcal{D}_\ell$ containing k documents is retrieved by nearest neighbour search. During this search, we do not allow single documents to be retrieved more than once at multiple layers. More formally, given a question $\mathbf{x}_0$ during testing time, the optimal parameters $\boldsymbol{\phi}^\star$ obtained by training and the query vector $\mathbf{q}_\ell = E_{Q,\ell}(\mathbf{x}_0; \boldsymbol{\theta}_{1:\ell}, \boldsymbol{\phi}_\ell^\star)$, the set of retrieved documents at layer ℓ is equal to

$$\mathcal{D}_\ell = \textit{NNSearch}(\mathbf{q}_\ell, \mathcal{D}_{1:\ell-1}, k) \quad (4)$$

where *NNSearch* returns the k nearest neighbours of $\mathbf{q}_\ell$ that are not included in the document sets $\mathcal{D}_{1:\ell-1}$ retrieved in previous layers. We use the Faiss-library for the implementation of *NNSearch* (Johnson et al., 2019). We investigated the performance on both exhaustive search on a flat index and the compressed IVF index (see section 4.2 for details).

With L layers, a total of $L \times k$ documents are retrieved. These retrieved documents are fed to the reader, together with the question $\mathbf{x}_0$, to obtain the answer. For the reader, we implement the state-of-the-art Fusion-in-Decoder (FiD) of (Izacard and Grave, 2021). Compared to other reader such as DPR-reader (Karpukhin et al., 2020) and REALM-reader (Guu et al., 2020) the FiD reader takes the retrieved document collection as an input simultaneously which allows to exploit the correlation between documents.

In a subset of experiments (e.g. Figure 3), we isolate retrieval in individual layers. In this case, each experiment retrieves from a single layer, without excluding any document.

4 Results

In the following, we evaluate how FetcHR influences the performance of modern readers and present isolated retrieval results of FetcHR.

4.1 Datasets

We test FetcHR on two commonly used open-domain question answering datasets:

- **WebQuestions** (Berant et al., 2013): This dataset includes questions collected using the Google Suggest API, with answers being entities from Freebase annotated by Mechanical Turk. Since only pairs of questions and answers are provided and no positive document, we follow (Karpukhin et al., 2020) by using the highest-ranked document from BM25 containing the answer span as positive document $\mathbf{d}^+$.
- **Natural Question** (Kwiatkowski et al., 2019): This dataset contains questions asked by users of Google-Search, with answers given as spans of text within Wikipedia articles. For each question, the positive document is the Wikipedia article containing the span with the answer.

The pre-processed English Wikipedia dump from December 2018 is used as the document memory as provided by (Karpukhin et al., 2020). This Wikipedia dump has been divided into non-overlapping chunks of 100 words following (Chen et al., 2017) and (Wang et al., 2019). Each chunk corresponds to a document. In total, there are $21,015,324$ documents.

4.2 Implementation Details

Hardware and libraries We use 32 Nvidia RTX 3090 GPUs with a total memory of 768 GB for training and testing of FetcHR. The distributed training is implemented in PyTorch with NCCL backend (Paszke et al., 2019). Our model implementation is is based on the Huggingface Transformers library (Wolf et al., 2020). The training time of the FetcHR retriever is $30-50$ hours for all our experiments. For training the FiD-large reader, we use a single Nvidia RTX A6000 GPU with 48 GB of RAM and gradient accumulation over 32 steps. This training takes about 100 hours.

Dataset details We follow the train/test splits from (Karpukhin et al., 2020) and we discard datapoints when the gold documents don't match the applied Wikipedia dump. This filtering process leaves us with a train set of 122,892 data points, which come from Natural Question, TriviaQA, WebQuestions, and CuratedTREC.

Training details We initialize the model parameters using the multiset checkpoint that was trained and provided by DPR. For the contrastive loss function, we use in-batch negatives. Our total training time is 30 epochs. The learning rate is $2 \cdot 10^{-5}$, and we use Adam optimizer (Kingma and Ba, 2014), linear scheduling with warm-up, and a dropout rate of 0.1. Our batch size is 256. We evaluate two checkpoints after training: the one with the lowest validation loss and the last checkpoint. The best performing checkpoint is reported in this paper. For distributing the training over multiple GPUs, we compute the scores on each GPU first and gather these scores to compute the loss. Then, we reduce the loss back to each GPU and compute local gradients. The final gradient update is averaged over all local gradients.

Retrieval and search In the nearest neighbor search function "NNSearch", documents that have already been retrieved are excluded by iteratively increasing $k \to k'$ until k new documents are retrieved. The underlying search algorithm uses the Faiss library. However, due to computational limitations, in most experiments, we use an IVF search index with 131072 clusters and 128 inference probes. We end-to-end ran experiments using both the IVF index and a flat index for exhaustive search. The IVF index was built on four Nvidia RTX 3090 GPUs that sums up to 96 GB VRAM. During inference, we ran IVF and flat index on CPU with access to 2 TB of physical memory. The total search time required for FetcHR is about 0.5 s on IVF index and 150 s on the flat index for a single inference.

4.3 Baselines

We compare FetcHR with DPR (Karpukhin et al., 2020) by testing it on the state-of-the-art Fusion-in-Decoder reader (FiD, (Izacard and Grave, 2021)). DPR is the best performing retriever in the original FiD publication and serves as a strong baseline.

The authors of DPR published multiple checkpoints of their work, some of which are trained on a single dataset (Natural Question) while others are trained on multiple datasets (Natural Question, TriviaQA, WebQuestions, CuratedTrec). We compare with the checkpoint trained on multiple dataset, which also serves as initialization of our model. For a fair comparison, we re-evaluate the DPR checkpoint on the same search index (IVF and flat), with identical retrieval budget $L \times k$, identical tokenization and entity normalization. Retrieved documents are fed to the FiD reader with pre-trained weights, as provided by the authors. We use the Fusion-in-Decoder in either base or large configuration. Fusion-in-decoder was trained on the Natural Question, TriviaQA and SQuAD v1.1 on 100 retrieved documents. We finetuned FiD-large to read from 240 documents from the Natural Question train set for 1 epoch. For the WebQuestion dataset, we performed an additional finetuning of the previously obtained Natural Question checkpoint to compensate for the small size of the WebQuestion dataset. We stopped this finetuning after 15 epochs. We denote the finetuned checkpoints as *FiD-large trained* in our tables.

4.4 Performance Metrics

Since the critical occurrence is a qualitatively metric which cannot be measured automatically, we follow the standard convention of retrieval accuracy and exact match from related work to measure the performance of our model as follows:

Retrieval Accuracy The retrieval accuracy is the probability that the correct answer span is included in one of the documents that are retrieved. Normalizations are performed, such as lower casing as well as removing punctuation and articles. This accuracy is commonly used to evaluate retrieval systems but is not capturing the occurrence of critical features in the retrieved document collection (see Figure 1).

Exact Match The performance of a reader is measured by the exact match (EM) score. This score is calculated by the percentage of exact matches between the reader's output and the correct answer. This score provides an end-to-end QA score capturing also the occurrence of critical features in the document collection.

4.5 Main Results

Figure 3 illustrates the retrieval accuracy of single FetcHR layer. We consider retrieval budgets of $L \times k = 10$ and $L \times k = 120$ and compare

Retriever	NQ		WebQ	
	top-120	top-240	top-120	top-240
DPR-IVFIdx	81.7	83.8	81.6	83.4
FetcHR-IVFIdx	**83.9**	**85.6**	**82.5**	**84.4**
DPR-flat	**86.5**	**88.2**	**85.2**	**87.3**
FetcHR-flat	**86.5**	**88.2**	84.8	86.8

Table 1: Top-120 and -240 accuracy's for different retriever on a flat and a compressed search space (IVFIdx).

Retriever	FiD-base		FiD-large				FiD-large trained	
	top-120 NQ	top-240 NQ	top-120 NQ	top-240 NQ	top-120 WebQ	top-240 WebQ	top-240 NQ	top-240 WebQ
DPR-IVFIdx	41.0	41.5	45.7	46.4	24.9	26.2	46.6	36.9
FetcHR-IVFIdx	**43.7**	**43.7**	**48.1**	**49.3**	**26.1**	**27.2**	**48.7**	**39.9**
DPR-flat	46.0	46.0	50.5	51.3	27.0	28.1	51.6	40.7
FetcHR-flat	**46.7**	**46.6**	**50.8**	**52.0**	**27.1**	**28.2**	**53.3**	**48.0**

Table 2: Exact-match scores with different readers on Natural Question and WebQuestion test sets.

the results to DPR which always retrieves at the final output layer 12. In contrast to the rest of this work, where FetcHR retrieves from all/multiple layers simultaneously ($L > 1$), in this experiment we retrieve from individual layers separately and independently ($L = 1$). Figure 3 reveals that the retrieval accuracy improves as the layer becomes deeper. The final layer achieves the best performance, while none of the FetchHR-layers outperforms DPR on its own, despite the last FetchHR-layer reaches nearly the same accuracy as DPR.

In the second experiment, we show that retrieving from all layers simultaneously achieves higher performance than the best individual layer, for an equal total number of retrieved documents. With $L = 12$ layers and $k = \{10, 20\}$, we consider total budgets of $L \times k = 120$ and $L \times k = 240$, respectively. We combine all retrieved documents as described in Section 3.4. The results are shown in Table 1. FetcHR's accuracy using all layers is higher than DPR when the IVF index is used. However, it is equal or slightly worse when the flat index is used. This might be a consequence of FetcHR being able to explore a compressed search space efficiently. While retrieval accuracy of FetcHR is not better than DPR for the flat index, in the next experiment we find that FetcHR performance is always higher when integrated into a QA system containing a reader to generate the answer.

We apply the Fusion-in-Decoder, a state-of-the-art reader, in the third experiment. This reader takes the retrieved documents combined with the input question as input and generates the answer. The exact match score is shown in Table 2 for question-answering tasks from the Natural Question and Web Question datasets. The documents provided by FetcHR always enable the reader to score higher than with the documents provided by DPR for all datasets and documents budgets. This is especially significant for the IVF index and the finetuned FiD reader, but it holds consistently also for the other scenarios, despite the lower retrieval performance shown in Table 1. These results confirm that the FetcHR document collection is superior compared to the DPR documents for QA tasks. We conclude that this improvement is due to a higher occurrence of critical features of the input question in the retrieved document collection. Figure 1 showcase three example questions with their corresponding occurrence of features in the retrieved document collection. We observe FetcHR to particular improve on the critical feature.

Table 3 provides a broader comparison of the performance of FetcHR to prior work on QA tasks. We consider prior work where retriever and reader are trained separately from the same or a strong overlapping dataset as with FetcHR. We find that FetcHR outperforms prior work when the FiD reader is finetuned on the FetcHR output distribution by 1.9 EM score on Natural Question and 2.1 EM score on Web Question.

Closed-book QA Models	NQ	WebQ
T5-base (Roberts et al., 2020)	25.7	28.2
T5-large (Roberts et al., 2020)	27.3	29.5
T5-XXL (Roberts et al., 2020)	32.8	35.6
GPT-3 (Brown et al., 2020)	29.9	41.5
Open-book QA Models	**NQ**	**WebQ**
BM25+BERT (Lee et al., 2019)	26.5	21.3
QRQA (Lee et al., 2019)	33.3	30.1
DPR (Karpukhin et al., 2020)	41.5	42.4
ReConsider-base (Iyer et al., 2020)	43.1	44.4
ReConsider-large (Iyer et al., 2020)	44.5	45.9
RETRO 7.5B w. DPR (Borgeaud et al., 2021)	45.5	-
FiD-base (Izacard and Grave, 2021)	48.2	-
FiD-large (Izacard and Grave, 2021)	51.4	-
FetcHR-flat / FiD-large trained	**53.3**	**48.0**

Table 3: EM scores of related work compared to our results on the Natural Question and WebQuestion test sets.

4.6 Ablations

Importance of FetcHR layers We investigate the importance of individual FetchHR layers when retrieving simultaneously from all layers. If some layers retrieve better documents than others, then we may consider the opportunity of unbalancing the contribution of different layers, i.e. letting those layers retrieve more documents than the others. We analyse individual layer performance by measuring the averaged amount of documents containing the answer span each layer retrieves additional to previous layers – we call this support in the following. Note that this support is different to Figure 3, where retrieval is performed in single layers while here retrieval is done in all layers. The results are illustrated in Figure 4. In this case, $k = 10$ and the total budget is $L \times k = 120$. The majority of correct documents is retrieved in the first layer but we observe that each layer has a significant contribution to the final retrieval performance showing the benefit of retrieving in multiple layers. We also observe that the middle layers have the lowest support. This low support could be a consequence of having a strong overlap of retrieved documents to previous layers sides while the first and last layer retrieve very different documents due to the largest difference in the hidden state representation of the input question.

Distribution of retrieval budget over multiple layers Given the results of Figure 4, we investigate alternative ways of dividing the total budget of documents $L \times k$ among the FetcHR layers, different from distributing the budget uniformly. Table 4 provides an overview of the retrieval accuracy in different configurations ranging from retrieval in the last layer only, the first and last layer, up to all layers. Note that the total amount of retrieved documents is 120 for all experiments. From these results, we conclude that the best configuration is when retrieval is distributed over all layers equally (i.e. $L = 12$, $k = 10$).

5 Conclusion

5.1 Summary

We presented retrieval-augmented transformers, a multi-encoder retrieval system exploiting different hierarchical abstractions of a model input. Our experiments show a competitive retrieval performance and a superior reader performance for two benchmark tasks on the FiD reader.

Since FetcHR is a retrieval system, it does not generate answers by itself and it requires a reader that can process the retrieved documents. We found that the FiD reader, in large configuration, is able to process retrieved documents efficiently – without additional training. Additional training of the FiD reader on the output distribution of FetcHR improved the performance even further and outperforms related work.

5.2 Discussion and Future Work

Our work shows that in the scenario of an end-to-end question answering task, a high retrieval

FetcHR layers	k per layer	accuracy
12	120	81.3
$1, 12$	60	82.6
$1, 6, 12$	40	83.1
$1, 2, 3, 10, 11, 12$	20	83.4
$2, 4, 6, 8, 10, 12$	20	83.5
$1, 2, 3, 4, 5, 6, 7, 8, 9, 10, 11, 12$	10	83.9

Table 4: Retrieval accuracy on Natural Question with varying distributions of L and k for a retrieval budget. Note that the total budget $L \times k = 120$ is kept constant across different rows of the table.

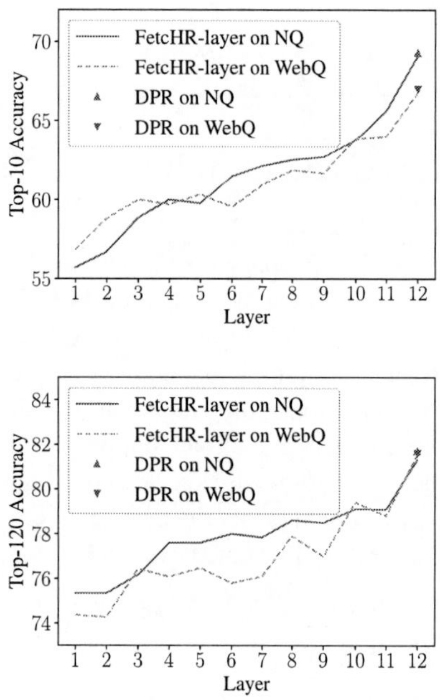

Figure 3: Top-10 (top) and top-120 (bottom) retrieval accuracy when all documents are retrieved in a single FetcHR layer compared to DPR. We evaluated this performance on the test set of Natural Questions. The accuracy is measured as percentage of top-k retrieved documents containing the correct answer span.

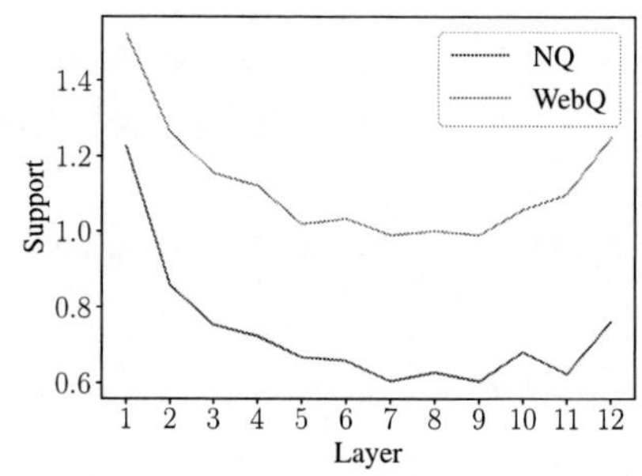

Figure 4: Support of each FetcHR layer to the final retrieval performance.

accuracy does not always translate to a high EM score of the reader output. We observe a better EM score of the reader despite an equal/slightly worse retrieval accuracy of the retriever. This appears to be contra-intuitive. However, a generative reader such as FiD performs inference over all retrieved documents at the same time. Typically, the answer to a question appears multiple times within the retrieved document collection. We believe this document distribution to be better, when the critical features of questions occur more often (see Figure 1). This might lead to future work aiming to develop automated metrics for retrieval systems when end-to-end question answering is the goal.

Another interesting observation is that FetcHR obtains the largest improvement in many scenarios on a compressed IVF index. We believe this is influenced by a wider exploration of the compressed search space, in addition to the hierarchical retrieval. This wider exploration might be a consequence of different queries from the individual FetcHR layers.

FetcHR demonstrated that a well performing retriever can be obtained with a query encoder build from just a few transformer-layers. With just a single transformer-layer and an attached retrieval network, we obtained decent retrieval performance. In the future, this may allow more hardware-efficient inference, shifting computational needs from the transformer network to the nearest neighbour search method. In future work, end-to-end training methods of FetcHR with FiD might lead to a fusion language model with both parametric and non-parametric knowledge over multiple layers. We believe this will have a significant impact on knowledge-intense tasks.

6 Limitations

Despite being trainable and usable for most datasets and document memories, there are some limitations to consider. The first one is related to the retrieval index. The discussed flat retrieval index scales poorly to large document memories. Despite being commonly used in research publications, the practical application of flat indices is limited due to long inference times on large document memories. Due to the poor scaling of the flat index, we also presented results on the much fast and more scalable IVFIndex. Another limitation is related to the DPR retriever as initial checkpoint for the retriever. We found very good retrieval results when FetcHR is trained on one of the pretraining datasets for DPR, however we observed a performance drop when FetcHR is used on a novel dataset. As this drop is expected for most models when train and test data distribution are not matching, a solution to this is an additional training of DPR following the DPR approach on the new dataset first. Afterwards, the presented FetcHR training can be conducted.

Ethics Statement

FetcHR shares the same ethical considerations and societal impact as prior work on language models and retrieval systems. Even though FetcHR improves performance on knowledge-intense tasks, it inherits the bias given by the training data and the collection of documents in the memory. This bias might lead to unfair or misleading model outputs. Since FetcHR does not have an explicit mechanism to detect and prevent a manipulated document memory, it could get prone to retrieve documents containing fake knowledge.

References

Petr Baudiš and Jan Šedivỳ. 2015. Modeling of the question answering task in the yodaqa system. In *International Conference of the Cross-Language Evaluation Forum for European Languages*, pages 222–228. Springer.

Jonathan Berant, Andrew Chou, Roy Frostig, and Percy Liang. 2013. Semantic parsing on freebase from question-answer pairs. In *Proceedings of the 2013 conference on empirical methods in natural language processing*, pages 1533–1544.

Sebastian Borgeaud, Arthur Mensch, Jordan Hoffmann, Trevor Cai, Eliza Rutherford, Katie Millican, George van den Driessche, Jean-Baptiste Lespiau, Bogdan Damoc, Aidan Clark, et al. 2021. Improving language models by retrieving from trillions of tokens. *arXiv preprint arXiv:2112.04426*.

Tom Brown, Benjamin Mann, Nick Ryder, Melanie Subbiah, Jared D Kaplan, Prafulla Dhariwal, Arvind Neelakantan, Pranav Shyam, Girish Sastry, Amanda Askell, et al. 2020. Language models are few-shot learners. *Advances in neural information processing systems*, 33:1877–1901.

Danqi Chen, Adam Fisch, Jason Weston, and Antoine Bordes. 2017. Reading wikipedia to answer open-domain questions. In *55th Annual Meeting of the Association for Computational Linguistics, ACL 2017*, pages 1870–1879. Association for Computational Linguistics (ACL).

Jacob Devlin, Ming-Wei Chang, Kenton Lee, and Kristina Toutanova. 2019. Bert: Pre-training of deep bidirectional transformers for language understanding. In *Proceedings of NAACL-HLT*, pages 4171–4186.

Utku Evci, Vincent Dumoulin, Hugo Larochelle, and Michael C Mozer. 2022. Head2toe: Utilizing intermediate representations for better transfer learning. In *International Conference on Machine Learning*, pages 6009–6033. PMLR.

Kelvin Guu, Kenton Lee, Zora Tung, Panupong Pasupat, and Mingwei Chang. 2020. Retrieval augmented language model pre-training. In *International Conference on Machine Learning*, pages 3929–3938. PMLR.

Srinivasan Iyer, Sewon Min, Yashar Mehdad, and Wen-tau Yih. 2020. Reconsider: Re-ranking using span-focused cross-attention for open domain question answering. *arXiv preprint arXiv:2010.10757*.

Gautier Izacard and Edouard Grave. 2021. Leveraging passage retrieval with generative models for open domain question answering. In *EACL 2021-16th Conference of the European Chapter of the Association for Computational Linguistics*, pages 874–880. Association for Computational Linguistics.

Jeff Johnson, Matthijs Douze, and Hervé Jégou. 2019. Billion-scale similarity search with gpus. *IEEE Transactions on Big Data*.

Mandar Joshi, Eunsol Choi, Daniel S Weld, and Luke Zettlemoyer. 2017. Triviaqa: A large scale distantly supervised challenge dataset for reading comprehension. *arXiv preprint arXiv:1705.03551*.

Vladimir Karpukhin, Barlas Oguz, Sewon Min, Patrick Lewis, Ledell Wu, Sergey Edunov, Danqi Chen, and Wen-tau Yih. 2020. Dense passage retrieval for open-domain question answering. In *Proceedings of the 2020 Conference on Empirical Methods in Natural Language Processing (EMNLP)*, pages 6769–6781.

Omar Khattab and Matei Zaharia. 2020. Colbert: Efficient and effective passage search via contextualized late interaction over bert. In *Proceedings of the 43rd International ACM SIGIR conference on research and development in Information Retrieval*, pages 39–48.

Diederik P Kingma and Jimmy Ba. 2014. Adam: A method for stochastic optimization. *arXiv preprint arXiv:1412.6980*.

Tom Kwiatkowski, Jennimaria Palomaki, Olivia Redfield, Michael Collins, Ankur Parikh, Chris Alberti, Danielle Epstein, Illia Polosukhin, Jacob Devlin, Kenton Lee, et al. 2019. Natural questions: a benchmark for question answering research. *Transactions of the Association for Computational Linguistics*, 7:453–466.

Kenton Lee, Ming-Wei Chang, and Kristina Toutanova. 2019. Latent retrieval for weakly supervised open domain question answering. In *Proceedings of the 57th Annual Meeting of the Association for Computational Linguistics*, pages 6086–6096.

Patrick Lewis, Ethan Perez, Aleksandra Piktus, Fabio Petroni, Vladimir Karpukhin, Naman Goyal, Heinrich Küttler, Mike Lewis, Wen-tau Yih, Tim Rocktäschel, et al. 2020. Retrieval-augmented generation for knowledge-intensive nlp tasks. *Advances in Neural Information Processing Systems*, 33:9459–9474.

Yi Luan, Jacob Eisenstein, Kristina Toutanova, and Michael Collins. 2021. Sparse, dense, and attentional representations for text retrieval. *Transactions of the Association for Computational Linguistics*, 9:329–345.

Sewon Min, Danqi Chen, Hannaneh Hajishirzi, and Luke Zettlemoyer. 2019. A discrete hard em approach for weakly supervised question answering. *arXiv preprint arXiv:1909.04849*.

Yifan Nie, Yanling Li, and Jian-Yun Nie. 2018a. Empirical study of multi-level convolution models for ir based on representations and interactions. *Proceedings of the 2018 ACM SIGIR International Conference on Theory of Information Retrieval*.

Yifan Nie, Alessandro Sordoni, and Jian-Yun Nie. 2018b. Multi-level abstraction convolutional model with weak supervision for information retrieval. *The 41st International ACM SIGIR Conference on Research & Development in Information Retrieval*.

Yixin Nie, Songhe Wang, and Mohit Bansal. 2019. Revealing the importance of semantic retrieval for machine reading at scale. In *Proceedings of the 2019 Conference on Empirical Methods in Natural Language Processing and the 9th International Joint Conference on Natural Language Processing (EMNLP-IJCNLP)*, pages 2553–2566.

Adam Paszke, Sam Gross, Francisco Massa, Adam Lerer, James Bradbury, Gregory Chanan, Trevor Killeen, Zeming Lin, Natalia Gimelshein, Luca Antiga, et al. 2019. Pytorch: An imperative style, high-performance deep learning library. *Advances in neural information processing systems*, 32.

Yingqi Qu, Yuchen Ding, Jing Liu, Kai Liu, Ruiyang Ren, Wayne Xin Zhao, Daxiang Dong, Hua Wu, and Haifeng Wang. 2021. Rocketqa: An optimized training approach to dense passage retrieval for open-domain question answering. In *Proceedings of the 2021 Conference of the North American Chapter of the Association for Computational Linguistics: Human Language Technologies*, pages 5835–5847.

Adam Roberts, Colin Raffel, and Noam Shazeer. 2020. How much knowledge can you pack into the parameters of a language model? In *Proceedings of the 2020 Conference on Empirical Methods in Natural Language Processing (EMNLP)*, pages 5418–5426.

Anna Rogers, Olga Kovaleva, and Anna Rumshisky. 2020. A primer in bertology: What we know about how bert works. *Transactions of the Association for Computational Linguistics*, 8:842–866.

Devendra Singh, Siva Reddy, Will Hamilton, Chris Dyer, and Dani Yogatama. 2021. End-to-end training of multi-document reader and retriever for open-domain question answering. *Advances in Neural Information Processing Systems*, 34.

Ellen M Voorhees et al. 1999. The trec-8 question answering track report. In *Trec*, volume 99, pages 77–82.

Zhiguo Wang, Patrick Ng, Xiaofei Ma, Ramesh Nallapati, and Bing Xiang. 2019. Multi-passage bert: A globally normalized bert model for open-domain question answering. In *Proceedings of the 2019 Conference on Empirical Methods in Natural Language Processing and the 9th International Joint Conference on Natural Language Processing (EMNLP-IJCNLP)*, pages 5878–5882.

Thomas Wolf, Lysandre Debut, Victor Sanh, Julien Chaumond, Clement Delangue, Anthony Moi, Pierric Cistac, Tim Rault, Remi Louf, Morgan Funtowicz, et al. 2020. Transformers: State-of-the-art natural language processing. In *Proceedings of the 2020 Conference on Empirical Methods in Natural Language Processing: System Demonstrations*, pages 38–45.

Tomer Wolfson, Mor Geva, Ankit Gupta, Matt Gardner, Yoav Goldberg, Daniel Deutch, and Jonathan Berant. 2020. Break it down: A question understanding benchmark. *Transactions of the Association for Computational Linguistics*, 8:183–198.

Wei Yang, Yuqing Xie, Aileen Lin, Xingyu Li, Luchen Tan, Kun Xiong, Ming Li, and Jimmy Lin. 2019. End-to-end open-domain question answering with bertserini. In *Proceedings of the 2019 Conference of the North American Chapter of the Association for Computational Linguistics (Demonstrations)*, pages 72–77.

Wen-tau Yih, Kristina Toutanova, John C Platt, and Christopher Meek. 2011. Learning discriminative projections for text similarity measures. In *Proceedings of the fifteenth conference on computational natural language learning*, pages 247–256.

Shun Zhang, Yaobo Liang, Ming Gong, Daxin Jiang, and Nan Duan. 2022. Multi-view document representation learning for open-domain dense retrieval. In *ACL*.

A Datasets

The datasets used in this work are open-source and widely used in the community. We make use of a preprocessed and published version by (Karpukhin et al., 2020) which can be downloaded from here: `https://github.com/facebookresearch/DPR`. In Table 5 the statistics of these datasets can be found.

Natural Question (Kwiatkowski et al., 2019)
URL: `https://ai.google.com/research/NaturalQuestions/download`
License: `https://github.com/google-research-datasets/natural-questions/blob/master/LICENSE`

WebQuestions (Berant et al., 2013)
URL: `https://github.com/google-research/language/tree/master/language/orqa#getting-the-data`
License: `https://nlp.stanford.edu/software/sempre/`

TriviaQA (Joshi et al., 2017)
URL: `http://nlp.cs.washington.edu/triviaqa/`
License: `https://github.com/mandarjoshi90/triviaqa/blob/master/LICENSE`

CuratedTrec (Baudiš and Šedivý, 2015)
URL: `https://github.com/brmson/dataset-factoid-curated`
License: `https://github.com/brmson/dataset-factoid-curated/tree/master/trec`

Dataset	Filtered Train	Development	Test
Natural Questions	58,880	8,758	3,610
WebQuestions	2,474	8,837	2,032
TriviaQA	60,413	361	11,313
CuratedTREC	1,125	133	694

Table 5: Datasets used in this work.

An Entity-based Claim Extraction Pipeline for Real-world Biomedical Fact-checking

Amelie Wührl, Lara Grimminger, and **Roman Klinger**
Institut für Maschinelle Sprachverarbeitung, University of Stuttgart, Germany
{amelie.wuehrl, lara.grimminger, roman.klinger}@ims.uni-stuttgart.de

Abstract

Existing fact-checking models for biomedical claims are typically trained on synthetic or well-worded data and hardly transfer to social media content. This mismatch can be mitigated by adapting the social media input to mimic the focused nature of common training claims. To do so, Wührl and Klinger (2022a) propose to extract concise claims based on medical entities in the text. However, their study has two limitations: First, it relies on gold-annotated entities. Therefore, its feasibility for a real-world application cannot be assessed since this requires detecting relevant entities automatically. Second, they represent claim entities with the original tokens. This constitutes a terminology mismatch which potentially limits the fact-checking performance. To understand both challenges, we propose a claim extraction pipeline for medical tweets that incorporates named entity recognition and terminology normalization via entity linking. We show that automatic NER does lead to a performance drop in comparison to using gold annotations but the fact-checking performance still improves considerably over inputting the unchanged tweets. Normalizing entities to their canonical forms does, however, not improve the performance.

1 Introduction

Fact-checking models trained on synthetic, well-worded and atomic claims struggle to transfer to colloquial content (Kim et al., 2021). There are multiple ways to address this problem: We can build custom datasets and models that verify medical content shared online (Saakyan et al., 2021; Mohr et al., 2022; Sarrouti et al., 2021) and tackle related tasks (Sundriyal et al., 2022; Dougrez-Lewis et al., 2022). Alternatively, we can adapt the input before addressing other fact-checking tasks. Bhatnagar et al. (2022) create claim summaries and find that this improves the detection of previously fact-checked claims. Similarly, Wührl and Klinger (2022a) extract concise claims from user-generated text in an effort to mimic the focused, well-structured nature of the claims the fact-checking models were originally trained on. They find that this improves the accuracy of pre-trained evidence-based fact-checking models in the biomedical domain.

	Claim	Evidence
orig	medicines causes blood clots	drospirenone may significantly increase chances of developing venous thromboembolic events
norm	pharmaceutical preparations causes thrombus	

Table 1: Example claim represented with original and normalized entities together with evidence.

However, the study by Wührl and Klinger (2022a) is limited in two ways: (1) Their claim extraction method relies on gold-annotated, claim-related entities. For a realistic evaluation, such an oracle needs to be replaced by an entity recognizer. Only then it is possible measure the impact of potential error propagation which may ultimately render the method unfeasible. (2) The claim entities are represented by the original token sequence. This is problematic as medical mentions on Twitter potentially contain imprecise, abbreviated, or colloquial terminology. This is in contrast to the terminology in the original model input as well as the documents that we provide as evidence (cf. Table 1). We hypothesize that for a successful fact-check we need to close this gap by normalizing medical terminology in the input. Previous work suggested leveraging entity linking for evidence retrieval (Nooralahzadeh and Øvrelid, 2018; Taniguchi et al., 2018; Hanselowski et al., 2018) leading us to believe that it could also be beneficial for aligning claim and evidence.

We address both limitations and evaluate a real-world, fully-automatic claim extraction pipeline for medical tweets which incorporates an entity rec-

Proceedings of the Sixth Fact Extraction and VERification Workshop (FEVER), pages 29–37
May 5, 2023 ©2023 Association for Computational Linguistics

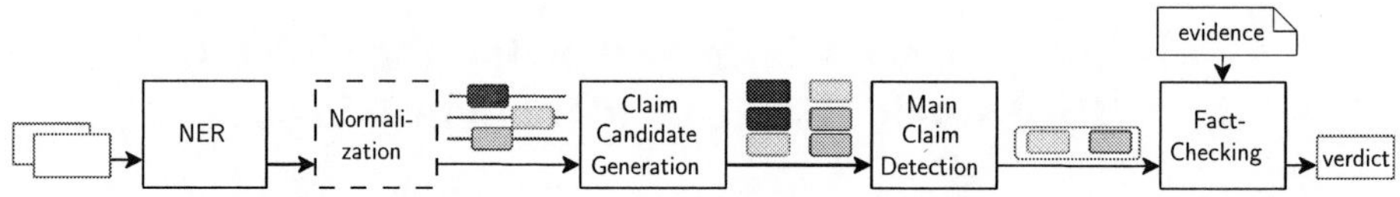

Figure 1: Overview of the claim extraction pipeline. Input documents go through entity recognition (NER), normalization, claim candidate generation, main claim detection and fact-checking. Colored boxes represent the entities which we use to extract claim candidates. Note that we evaluate the normalization module separately from the evaluation of the rest of the pipeline (see §3).

ognizer. It only relies on the original text as input that contains the claim. We further evaluate the impact of an entity linker for normalizing entity mentions to canonical forms based on the Unified Medical Language System (UMLS, Bodenreider, 2004). Our pipeline improves the fact-checking performance over tasking models to check unchanged tweets. Normalizing entities to overcome the terminology mismatch does not improve fact-checking, potentially due to limitations of biomedical entity linking for social media.

2 Methods

Figure 1 visualizes our pipeline. It takes text as input and performs *named entity recognition* and optionally term *normalization* via entity linking. Each unique entity pair forms the building blocks for a potential claim (*claim candidate generation*). The *main claim detection* identifies the core claim among the candidates that presumably represents the most important aspect of the text. The resulting claim is the input to the fact-checker. In our setting, we assume this to be a frozen pre-trained fact-checking model. We describe the modules in the following and the fact-checker in Section 3.2.

NER. We use the SpaCy environment[1] to train a custom NER model that detects medical entities. This framework relies on a transition-based parser (Lample et al., 2016) to predict entities in the input. In a preliminary study, we found that relying on an off-the-shelf model for biomedical NER, i.e., ScispaCy (Neumann et al., 2019), does not transfer to medical texts from social media. Refer to Appendix B.1 for a comparison of the two models.

Claim candidate generation. Wührl and Klinger (2022a) propose two extraction methods, i.e., $\text{condense}_{\text{seq}}$ and $\text{condense}_{\text{triple}}$. The first represents the claim as the token sequence from the first entity to the last entity, while the second relies on gold-annotated causal relations which they use to build the claims. We use the sequence method $\text{condense}_{\text{seq}}$ in our pipeline because both methods show on par performances (difference in 1pp F_1) and, in contrast to $\text{condense}_{\text{triple}}$, it does not require relation classification.

Following the $\text{condense}_{\text{seq}}$ method, we therefore extract the sequence from the character onset of the first entity to the character offset of the second entity for all pairs of entities found by the NER module.

Entity linking. To normalize entities, we use the *EntityLinking* component in ScispaCy (Neumann et al., 2019). This model compares an entity mention to concepts in an ontology and creates a ranked list of candidates, based on an approximate nearest neighbor search. For text normalization, we retrieve the canonical name of the top concept. For entities which could not be linked, we use the original mention instead. As the knowledge base, we use UMLS (Bodenreider, 2004).

Main claim detection. For tweets with more than two predicted entities, claim generation produces multiple claim candidates. To identify the claim to be passed to the fact-checking module, we train a text classifier to detect the main claim for a given input. We build on RoBERTArg[2], a RoBERTA-based text classification model trained to label input texts as ARGUMENT or NON-ARGUMENT. We fine-tune this model to classify texts as CLAIM VS. NON-CLAIM and to fit the social media health domain. At inference time, the claim candidate with the highest probability for the claim class constitutes the main claim. We refer to this as *ner+core-claim*.

3 Experiments

3.1 Data

CoVERT. We use the CoVERT dataset (Mohr et al., 2022) to test our pipeline. It consists of

[1] https://spacy.io/api/architectures#TransitionBasedParser

[2] https://huggingface.co/chkla/roberta-argument

	Input Claim														
	Gold entities							Fully automatic (Ours)							
	condense$_{seq}$				full tweets			ner+rand-ent-seq				ner+core-claim			
model	P	R	F_1	Δ_{full}	P	R	F_1	P	R	F_1	Δ_{full}	P	R	F_1	Δ_{full}
fever	83.3	1.9	3.7	+3.7	0.0	0.0	0.0	0.0	0.0	0.0	+0	100	0.4	0.8	+0.8
fever_sci	87.2	15.5	26.4	+18.4	91.7	4.2	8.0	92.3	4.7	9.0	+1.0	82.4	5.6	10.4	+2.4
scifact	90.9	7.6	14.0	+13.2	100	0.4	0.8	100	2.4	4.6	+3.8	100	2.4	4.7	+3.9
covidfact	55.6	28.4	37.6	+29.7	30.8	4.5	7.9	53.3	9.4	16.1	+8.2	58.1	14.3	23.0	+15.1
healthver	85.9	48.5	62.0	+16.8	82.8	31.1	45.2	75.6	23.2	35.5	−9.7	77.4	28.7	41.9	−3.3
average	80.6	20.4	28.7	+16.3	61.1	8.0	12.4	64.2	7.9	13.0	+0.6	83.6	10.1	16.2	+3.8

Table 2: Performance (precision, recall and F_1) of MultiVerS-based models (*fever, fever_sci, scifact, covidfact, healthver*) on CoVERT data. Model inputs are the full tweets, the entity-based sequence claims (condense$_{seq}$ (Wührl and Klinger, 2022a)), and claims from the fully automatic pipeline, *ner+rand-ent-seq* and *ner+core-claim*. Δ_{full} : difference in F_1 between the full tweet and performance for the respective input claim. We report the average across all models in the last row.

medical tweets labeled with fact-checking verdicts (SUPPORTS, REFUTES, NOT ENOUGH INFORMATION) and associated evidence texts. We follow the same filtering and preprocessing as Wührl and Klinger (2022a) which leaves us with 264 tweets. For 13 tweets, the NER model predicts only one or no entities. In these cases, we cannot generate claim candidates thus we can only consider 251 claims.

BEAR. We require an independent dataset to train the NER component. We find the BEAR dataset (Wührl and Klinger, 2022b) to be closest in domain and text type to the target data from CoVERT. BEAR provides 2100 tweets with a total of 6324 annotated medical entities from 14 entity classes. We use 80% of the data for training and 20% for testing the model.

Causal Claims. To build a classifier that identifies the core claims, we use the CAUSAL CLAIMS data from SemEval-2023 Task 8, Subtask 1.[3] It consists of medical Reddit posts and provides span-level annotations for *Claim*, *Experience*, *Experience based claim* and *Question*. Our goal is to differentiate claims from non-claims. Consequently, we extract all spans labeled as *Claim* and *Experience based claim* as positive instances for the claim class and use the remaining text spans as negative examples. This leads to 1704 claim and 6870 non-claim spans. We use a train/test split of 90/10%.

3.2 Evaluation

The fact-checking module serves as a by-proxy evaluation for the claim representations. Provided with a claim–evidence pair, the system predicts a fact-checking verdict that indicates if the evidence SUPPORTS or REFUTES the claim. We assume that the fact-checker is a frozen model for which we adapt the claim input. To gauge the checkability of a particular input, we compare the performance for predicting the correct verdict when the model is presented with claims of this type. This follows the evaluation in Wührl and Klinger (2022a).

The fact-checking models we employ stem from the MultiVerS architecture (Wadden et al., 2022).[4] This framework is designed for scientific fact-verification and provides five models (*fever, fever_sci, scifact, covidfact, healthver*), differing in training data. We report precision, recall and F_1 for predicting the correct fact-checking verdict (SUPPORTS, REFUTES, NOT ENOUGH INFORMATION) for a given claim-evidence pair.

3.3 Exp. 1: Impact of NER

In Exp. 1, we aim to understand the impact of automatic NER and main claim detection in the pipeline, instead of relying on gold-labeled entities.

Table 2 reports the results for our fully automatic claim extraction pipeline. Each column reports the performance for a specific type of input claim. *Full tweets* is the performance as reported by Wührl and Klinger (2022a) for the unchanged input tweets. The results denoted with condense$_{seq}$ describe their results with gold annotations, to which we compare. Our main results are in the last column (*ner+core-claim*). To understand the impact of the main claim detection, we compare against a purely random

[3] `https://causalclaims.github.io/`

[4] `https://github.com/dwadden/multivers`

selection of the main claim from all candidates in the tweet (*ner+rand-ent-seq*).

The rows correspond to the various fact-checking models. Δ columns report the difference in F_1 between the performance of checking the full tweet and the respective claim representation.

ner+core-claim shows an average performance of F_1 =16.2. The performance varies across the models. The *healthVer* model performs the best (41.9F_1). The average is considerably higher than using the full tweets (Δ=3.8 pp F_1). This improvement is consistent across all models, except for *healthVer*, presumably because it already shows a high performance for the original texts. To better understand the model behavior, we provide an analysis of its prediction in Appendix B.3. We see a particularly strong impact for the *covidfact* model, with Δ=15.1 pp. Despite this positive result, we see a performance drop when integrating entity recognition instead of building claim extraction on gold entity annotations. This decrease is not surprising since we expect some error propagation from an imperfect entity recognizer. Nevertheless, the results show that entity-based claim extraction also increases the fact-checking performance even under some error propagation throughout the real-world pipeline.

We further see that main claim detection is a required module – the performance for a randomly selected claim (*ner+rand-ent-seq*) is substantially lower. This indicates that using the same evidence and fact-checking model, not all potential claims in a tweet would receive the same verdict.

3.4 Exp. 2: Impact of Entity Normalization

In Exp. 2, we investigate if it is beneficial to assimilate the linguistic realizations of medical mentions to the expected input of the fact-checking models. More specifically, we suggest normalizing entity strings in the input. In contrast to Exp. 1, in which we evaluate the overall pipeline, we focus on the aspect of the entities here and therefore do not make use of the core claim detection method or the entity recognizer. Instead we build on top of gold annotations and, consequently, employ $\text{condense}_{\text{triple}}$ described in Section 2.

We use entity linking for term normalization and use ScispaCy's entity linking functionality with *en_core_sci_sm* as the underlying model (Neumann et al., 2019). For each (gold) entity, we use the canonical name of the concept with the highest linking score. Subsequently, we follow the $\text{condense}_{\text{triple}}$ method to represent claims.

	$\text{condense}_{\text{triple}}$ Claims					
	surface string			normalized ent.		
model	P	R	F_1	P	R	F_1
fever	81.8	3.4	6.5	75.0	1.1	2.2
fever_sci	89.8	20.1	32.8	93.9	11.7	20.9
scifact	86.4	7.2	13.3	94.4	6.4	12.1
covidfact	65.0	30.3	41.3	61.8	20.8	31.2
healthver	79.7	41.7	54.7	85.7	31.8	46.4
average	80.5	20.5	29.7	82.2	14.4	22.6

Table 3: Performance (precision, recall and F_1) of MultiVerS-based fact-checking models (*fever, fever_sci, scifact, covidfact, healthver*) on CoVERT claims built with non-normalized (surface string) vs. normalized entities. We report the average across all models in the last row.

Table 3 reports the results for claims built with non-normalized (*surface string*) vs. normalized entities (*normalized ent.*). The results indicated as $\text{condense}_{\text{triple}}$ *surface string* are analogue to the results in Wührl and Klinger (2022a). We see that normalization does not have the desired effect: The verdict prediction performance drops across all of the fact-checking models (from 29.7 to 22.6 in avg. F_1). We assume that this is, to a considerable extend, due to entity linking being a challenging task which leads to a limited performance of the employed linking module. We present an error analysis in Appendix B.4.

4 Conclusion & Future Work

We propose a fully automatic claim extraction pipeline that is capable of handling real-world medical content. We show that entity-based claim extraction has a positive effect on the performance of multiple fact-checking models – even after replacing the entity oracle with automatic NER. While we observe a negative impact of error propagation from NER and a performance drop as a result, fact-checking the extracted claims is more successful than checking unchanged tweets. Future research may therefore focus on improving the pipeline components as this clearly has the potential to further strengthen the verdict prediction performance. In particular, we expect an improved entity recognizer to have a considerable impact.

Our work focuses on the biomedical domain and builds upon the assumption by Wührl and Klinger (2022a) that claims in this domain are strongly centered around entities. Claims from other domains may share this property which could make entity-based claim extraction applicable for such claims as well. We leave the evaluation for future work.

We find that normalizing entity mentions does not improve the fact-checking performance. However, our analysis shows that the off-the-shelf linking module might be too unreliable. To fully gauge the potential of normalizing entities, future work needs to ensure correct mappings (creating gold links or building a reliable linker) before evaluating the downstream fact-checking performance.

Acknowledgments

This research has been conducted as part of the FIBISS project which is funded by the German Research Council (DFG, project number: KL 2869/5-1). We thank the anonymous reviewers for their valuable feedback.

Limitations

Our work focused on evaluating the impact of putting together a set of components to achieve a real-world system for fact-checking. For answering the research question at hand, the components offered themselves as appropriate choices. This being said, to some degree, the particular selection may limit the expressiveness of the experiments.

By instantiating the pipeline components with the set of models and underlying data that we chose, our findings are limited to this setting. However, the analysis that we provide in Appendix B dissects the pipeline results and allows us to draw more general conclusions about the impact of replacing individual components.

We propose that the main claim detection receives more attention in future research. This may mitigate the issue that this module is potentially the most in-transparent component. Compared to the NER, this task can be modeled in various ways. We rely on the output probabilities to identify the claim candidate the model is most confident about. While this is a straight-forward approach and we show that it works as intended, prediction probabilities – especially for deep models – may not always be a distinctive indicator of model confidence. To overcome this limitation, alternative ways of detecting the main claim should be evaluated.

Ethical Considerations

A real-world fact-checking pipeline presents itself as a valuable tool. However, we advise against using the pipeline purely automatically that at this point in time. Unless they are used hand-in-hand with a human expert performing or supervising the fact-check, such systems are not reliable enough yet.

Potential issues are the result of the inherent opaqueness of sophisticated automatic analysis pipelines. In the system that we propose, it is important that the impact of each module needs to explain itself to the user. While there is recent work on explainability particularly in the area of fact checking, this work did not yet focus on entity-based approaches. It is important that a user can clearly understand which claim in a statement is checked and which risks potential error propagation might lead to. Therefore, before deploying such systems for fully automatic filtering or labeling of problematic messages in a social media content, there needs to be more research on explainability and transparency of such systems.

References

Varad Bhatnagar, Diptesh Kanojia, and Kameswari Chebrolu. 2022. Harnessing abstractive summarization for fact-checked claim detection. In *Proceedings of the 29th International Conference on Computational Linguistics*, pages 2934–2945, Gyeongju, Republic of Korea. International Committee on Computational Linguistics.

Olivier Bodenreider. 2004. The unified medical language system (UMLS): integrating biomedical terminology. *Nucleic Acids Research*, 32:D267–270.

John Dougrez-Lewis, Elena Kochkina, Miguel Arana-Catania, Maria Liakata, and Yulan He. 2022. PHEMEPlus: Enriching social media rumour verification with external evidence. In *Proceedings of the Fifth Fact Extraction and VERification Workshop (FEVER)*, pages 49–58, Dublin, Ireland. Association for Computational Linguistics.

Andreas Hanselowski, Hao Zhang, Zile Li, Daniil Sorokin, Benjamin Schiller, Claudia Schulz, and Iryna Gurevych. 2018. UKP-athene: Multi-sentence textual entailment for claim verification. In *Proceedings of the First Workshop on Fact Extraction and VERification (FEVER)*, pages 103–108, Brussels, Belgium. Association for Computational Linguistics.

Byeongchang Kim, Hyunwoo Kim, Seokhee Hong, and Gunhee Kim. 2021. How robust are fact checking systems on colloquial claims? In *Proceedings of the 2021 Conference of the North American Chapter of the Association for Computational Linguistics: Human Language Technologies*, pages 1535–1548, Online. Association for Computational Linguistics.

Guillaume Lample, Miguel Ballesteros, Sandeep Subramanian, Kazuya Kawakami, and Chris Dyer. 2016. Neural architectures for named entity recognition. In *Proceedings of the 2016 Conference of the North American Chapter of the Association for Computational Linguistics: Human Language Technologies*, pages 260–270, San Diego, California. Association for Computational Linguistics.

Isabelle Mohr, Amelie Wührl, and Roman Klinger. 2022. CoVERT: A corpus of fact-checked biomedical COVID-19 tweets. In *Proceedings of the Thirteenth Language Resources and Evaluation Conference*, pages 244–257, Marseille, France. European Language Resources Association.

Mark Neumann, Daniel King, Iz Beltagy, and Waleed Ammar. 2019. ScispaCy: Fast and Robust Models for Biomedical Natural Language Processing. In *Proceedings of the 18th BioNLP Workshop and Shared Task*, pages 319–327, Florence, Italy. Association for Computational Linguistics.

Farhad Nooralahzadeh and Lilja Øvrelid. 2018. SIRIUS-LTG: An entity linking approach to fact extraction and verification. In *Proceedings of the First Workshop on Fact Extraction and VERification (FEVER)*, pages 119–123, Brussels, Belgium. Association for Computational Linguistics.

Arkadiy Saakyan, Tuhin Chakrabarty, and Smaranda Muresan. 2021. COVID-fact: Fact extraction and verification of real-world claims on COVID-19 pandemic. In *Proceedings of the 59th Annual Meeting of the Association for Computational Linguistics and the 11th International Joint Conference on Natural Language Processing (Volume 1: Long Papers)*, pages 2116–2129, Online. Association for Computational Linguistics.

Mourad Sarrouti, Asma Ben Abacha, Yassine Mrabet, and Dina Demner-Fushman. 2021. Evidence-based fact-checking of health-related claims. In *Findings of the Association for Computational Linguistics: EMNLP 2021*, pages 3499–3512, Punta Cana, Dominican Republic. Association for Computational Linguistics.

Megha Sundriyal, Atharva Kulkarni, Vaibhav Pulastya, Md Shad Akhtar, and Tanmoy Chakraborty. 2022. Empowering the fact-checkers! automatic identification of claim spans on twitter. In *Proceedings of the 2022 Conference on Empirical Methods in Natural Language Processing*, page 7701–7715, Abu Dhabi, United Arab Emirates. Association for Computational Linguistics.

Motoki Taniguchi, Tomoki Taniguchi, Takumi Takahashi, Yasuhide Miura, and Tomoko Ohkuma. 2018. Integrating entity linking and evidence ranking for fact extraction and verification. In *Proceedings of the First Workshop on Fact Extraction and VERification (FEVER)*, pages 124–126, Brussels, Belgium. Association for Computational Linguistics.

David Wadden, Kyle Lo, Lucy Lu Wang, Arman Cohan, Iz Beltagy, and Hannaneh Hajishirzi. 2022. MultiVerS: Improving scientific claim verification with weak supervision and full-document context. In *Findings of the Association for Computational Linguistics: NAACL 2022*, pages 61–76, Seattle, United States. Association for Computational Linguistics.

Amelie Wührl and Roman Klinger. 2022a. Entity-based claim representation improves fact-checking of medical content in tweets. In *Proceedings of the 9th Workshop on Argument Mining*, pages 187–198, Online and in Gyeongju, Republic of Korea. International Conference on Computational Linguistics.

Amelie Wührl and Roman Klinger. 2022b. Recovering patient journeys: A corpus of biomedical entities and relations on Twitter (BEAR). In *Proceedings of the Thirteenth Language Resources and Evaluation Conference*, pages 4439–4450, Marseille, France. European Language Resources Association.

A Implementation details

In the following, we provide implementation details for the individual model components described in Section 2.

A.1 Named Entity Recognition

In a preliminary experiment, we use a pre-trained model for biomedical NER, i.e., the *en_core_sci_sm* model by ScispaCy (Neumann et al., 2019), that was trained on scientific, biomedical and clinical text to identify sequences of biomedical entities. We find that the off-the-shelf model transfers poorly to our target data which stems from social media. We provide the evaluation results for this experiment in Appendix B.2.1. Therefore, we train a custom NER model in spaCy on the BEAR dataset. We create an empty model using spacy.blank() and pass the language ID "en" for English. We provide the train/test splits and configuration file we use to train the model which includes all settings and hyperparameters here: `https://tinyurl.com/bear-ner`

A.2 Main Claim Detection

We fine-tune RoBERTArg[5] to classify texts as CLAIM vs. NON-CLAIM using the Causal Claim data. We create a train-validation split of 85/15 %. We train for 5 epochs with a batch size of 16, 409

[5] `https://huggingface.co/chkla/roberta-argument`

training steps per epoch, 136 warmup steps and a weight decay of 0.01. We use the same learning rate that was used in fine-tuning the underlying RoBERTArg model, i.e., a learning rate of 2.3102e-06. We evaluate the model every 500 steps using the validation set. After training, we use the model with the best performance on the validation set to make a prediction for each claim candidate.

A.3 Entity linking

We use the *EntityLinking* component in ScispaCy (Neumann et al., 2019) and *en_core_sci_sm* as the underlying model[6]. For each entity, the model maps the mention to the associated concept within UMLS (Bodenreider, 2004). We include the option to resolve abbreviations and leave the other configuration parameters at their default values.

B Analysis

We provide an evaluation and analyses of individual pipeline components to better understand the capabilities of the modules.

B.1 Evaluation Setup

NER. Entity recognition consists of two subtasks: (a) identifying the span of an entity and (b) predicting the entity class. Consequently, we evaluate the NER component of our pipeline in two modes. In the *strict* mode, the entity span and the entity class have to be identical to the gold data. In the *relaxed* mode, the entity span has to be identical to the gold data, entity class labels is ignored.

Note that the off-the-shelf ScispaCy (Neumann et al., 2019) model that we compare against only labels the entity span and not the entity class. Therefore, we can only evaluate its performance in the *relaxed* mode.

Further note that we need to map certain entity classes between the CoVERT and the BEAR dataset. To align CoVERT with BEAR, we map *Medical Condition* to *med_C*, *Treatment* to *treat_therapy*, and *OTHER* to other, respectively. The CoVERT dataset further contains the class *Symptom/Side-effect*, which corresponds to the class *med_C* of the BEAR dataset. Therefore, we map the class *Symptom/Side-effect* to the class *med_C*. Entities which have been labeled in BEAR, but not in CoVERT, are ignored for the evaluation.

We report the macro-average of precision, recall and F_1 for both modes.

[6]https://allenai.github.io/scispacy/

Main claim detection. We evaluate the prediction of the model on the held-out test set from the CAUSAL CLAIM data. We report precision, recall and F_1 for both classes (CLAIM vs. NON-CLAIM) the as well as the macro-average.

B.2 Results

B.2.1 NER

We evaluate the performance of the NER component within our pipeline. Table 4 reports the results for the strict and relaxed evaluation mode. First, we evaluate the performance on the unseen test split of the BEAR data – the dataset we use for training the model. To gauge how well it transfers to our target data, we evaluate the performance for the entity predictions in CoVERT. We compare the performance of our custom model to the performance of the pre-trained ScispaCy model.

For the BEAR data, our model reaches an average F_1 of 0.41 for the strict evaluation mode. Note that in this mode only exact span and entity type matches count as true positives. If we relax this condition and disregard the entity type, the model achieves an F_1-score of 0.51. When moving to a slightly different type of input text, i.e., the CoVERT data, the average F_1-scores for the strict and relaxed evaluation modes reach 0.34 and 0.38, respectively.

Compared to our custom model, the performance of the off-the-shelf model from ScispaCy is much lower. For the relaxed mode, we observe a Δ in F_1 of 0.21 and 0.12 for the BEAR and CoVERT data, respectively. This showcases the necessity of a customized model for NER in this setting.

Overall, this evaluation of the entity recognition shows moderate performance. Importantly, the results also indicate that improving this component is likely to improve the overall fact-checking performance.

B.2.2 Main claim detection

We evaluate the performance of the claim detection model on the held-out test set. We report the results in Table 5. We can see that the model successfully differentiates claims from non-claims (F_1-scores of 0.94 and 0.99, respectively).

B.3 Analysis of *healthver* prediction

We want to understand why the *healthver* model behaves unexpectedly compared to the other models (refer to Table 2). We saw that providing the

model	eval. mode	target data BEAR P	R	F_1	CoVERT P	R	F_1
ScispaCy	strict	-	-	-	-	-	-
	relaxed	.2	.61	.3	.16	.72	.26
Ours	strict	.46	.37	.41	.26	.51	.34
	relaxed	.56	.46	.51	.29	.57	.38

Table 4: Evaluation of our NER module for the test split of the BEAR dataset and the CoVERT data. We report the macro average precision (P), recall (R) and F_1 across all entity classes. We report results for a strict and a relaxed evaluation mode. We compare against the performance of an off-the-shelf ScispaCy (Neumann et al., 2019) model (*en_core_sci_sm*). This model only labels the entity span, not the entity class. Therefore, we only evaluate in the relaxed mode.

class	P	R	F_1
Non-claim	0.98	0.99	0.99
Claim	0.95	0.93	0.94
macro av.	0.97	0.96	0.96

Table 5: Performance (precision (P), recall (R), F_1) of the claim detection model for CAUSAL CLAIMS test set.

automatically extracted claim leads to a slight performance decrease compared to inputting the full tweet, while the claims extracted using gold entities were more successfully checked. We hypothesize that for this model, the automatic extraction either removed relevant pieces of the input that it relied on previously for a successful prediction or it may have introduced irrelevant noise. Therefore, we compare the predictions of this model for our *ner+core-claim* inputs to the claims built on gold-labeled entities $\text{condense}_{\text{seq}}$. Note that we compare the predictions which are not necessarily in line with the gold label.

Label distribution. Table 6 reports the distribution of predicted labels for both input types. The NEI class increases substantially (115 to 158 predicted instances) while SUPPORT and REFUTE become less frequent. This indicates that the claims become less checkable as NEI means a lack of information to support or refute the claim.

Label flips. To better understand which instances cause the model to predict a different verdict, we present the number of label transitions between the predictions for the gold-labeled entity claims and the predictions for our pipeline claims (*ner+core-claim*) in Table 7. From those results we can observe that for a substantial amount of instances (161) the predicted label actually does not shift. For 90 instances, we observe a label shift.

input claim	# Predicted labels SUPPORT	REFUTE	NEI
gold entities	110	39	115
ner+core-claim	69	24	158

Table 6: Labels predicted by the *healthver* model for claims extracted using $\text{condense}_{\text{seq}}$ based on gold entities and our pipeline (*ner+core-claim*). Note that there are 13 claims more in the gold-entity setting compared to *ner+core-claim* inputs. These are cases for which the NER module predicted ≤ 1 entity.

Most notably, claims that were supported and refuted when inputting the gold-entity claims, get classified as NEI when we input our extracted claims (46 and 18, respectively). In an introspection of this transition type, we observe that in cases, the automatic pipeline failed to detect the main claim, potentially rendering the evidence useless. Refer to Claims 3 and 4 in Table 7 for examples.

Flipped verdicts (SUPPORTS to REFUTES or vice versa) are less frequent. We observe a total of 11 instances. Refer to Claims 1 and 2 in Table 7.

We observe 15 cases in which the label flips to the correct gold label when we input our claim as opposed to the gold-entity-based claim. In the manual introspection, we observe many cases in which the claim from the pipeline slightly extends the context compared to the gold entity claim. Refer to Claims 5 and 6 in Table 7 for two examples.

For cases with consistent labels, we find that many instances either are identical to the claim extracted using gold entities (see Table 7, Example 7a) or only small amounts of context is added (see Table 7, Ex. 8).

This being said, we also observe cases in which the gold-entity and our predicted claim do not overlap and yet, the verdict stays consistent (Ex. 7b). This emphasizes the need to further improve the main claim detection step and leads us to hypothesize that this module may be another reason for the limited performance of this model. It appears that the *healthver* model is particularly sensitive to this component being somewhat unreliable and error propagation in general.

B.4 Entity Linking

Number of established mappings. There are no gold annotated mappings for the medical entities

id	transition	# inst.	example: gold-ent-claim	example: ner+core-claim	gold
1	S-R	7	Oral contraceptives cause more blood clots	blood clots and nobody is doing anything about that!!! Like 1 per 1,000 compared to basically 1 per MILLION with the Covid vaccine	S
2	R-S	4	COVID-19 vaccines can cause side effects	Vaccine reactions are rare. Info about side effects	S
3	S-NEI	46	COVID-19 1) directly causes viral pneumonia	pneumonia 3) can result in intubation	S
4	R-NEI	18	5G causes covid	vaccines cause infertility & autism	R
5	NEI-S	12	live virus that causes covid-19	vaccines don't use the live virus that causes covid-19	S
6	NEI-R	3	masks cause plague	masks cause plague... fauci knows... masks promote bacteria... and not the good kind... sinus	R
7a	S-S	53	covid vaccine doesn't cause fertility issues	covid vaccine doesn't cause fertility issues	S
7b	S-S		all brands of the vaccine can cause problems	death rate of COVID is said to be 10%. It is probable that some vaccines	S
8	R-R	14	Wearing a mask does cause disease	Wearing a mask does cause disease, harm the immune system	R
9	NEI-NEI	94	Auto-Immune disease causes the white blood cells that normally protect your body from invaders to turn around and attack your cells, tissues and organs	Auto-Immune disease causes the white blood cells that normally protect your body	S

Table 7: Label transitions as predicted by the *healthver* model for claims extracted using condense$_{seq}$ based on gold entities (gold-ent-claim) and our pipeline (*ner+core-claim*). We provide example instances for each type of label transitions along with the gold label for the fact-checking verdict.

in the CoVERT dataset that would allow for a full evaluation. We therefore approximate one aspect of the quality of the entity linking module by analyzing the number of entities that are being linked to any concept in the first place. Out of 719 entity mentions the linking module established mappings for 495 instances (68.8 %). We provide insights from an error analysis in the following section.

Error analysis. We aim to understand the type of error patterns introduced by the entity linking module. We analyze predicted links for a randomly drawn sample of 25 entities. We manually categorize the predicted concepts with regard to four properties. Table 8 reports the results as well as examples. *correctly linked* instances are mapped to the appropriate concept within UMLS. *Incorrect but related link* include instances which are mapped incorrectly, but the concept is related. *incorrect and unrelated link* include cases in which the linking is incorrect and also unrelated.

The analysis shows that the majority of mentions are linked to the correct (15 out of 25 instances) or at least a related (6 out of 25 instances) UMLS concept. Four instances within our sample were mapped to an unrelated UMLS concept.

While the majority of cases within our sample

error type	#	mention	pred. concept
correctly linked	15	glandular fever	Infectious Mononucleosis
incorr., related	6	fibro flare	Fibromyalgia
incorr. & unrelated	4	COVID	Covi Anxiety Scale [...]

Table 8: Number of error types within a sample of 25 entities along with examples.

are normalized correctly, this module potentially introduces many errors. Note that as pointed out before about 30 % of entities are not linked and consequently not replaced at all. In addition, an incorrectly mapped and replaced mention, even if the concept might be closely related, may change the meaning of a claim drastically. Take the following example claim: 'COVID cause of breathlessness'. While *breathlessness* is correctly mapped to *dyspnea*, *COVID* is linked to and subsequently replaced by an unrelated concept: 'Covi Anxiety Scale Clinical Classification cause of dyspnea'. This leads us to believe that the unreliability of the linking module is the main reason why the verdict prediction performance for the normalized claims is comparably low.

Enhancing Information Retrieval in Fact Extraction and Verification

Daniel Guzman-Olivares[1] **Lara Quijano-Sanchez**[1] **Federico Liberatore**[2]
[1] Autonomous University of Madrid, Spain
[2] Cardiff University, United Kingdom
daniel.guzmano@estudiante.uam.es
lara.quijano@uam.es
liberatoref@cardiff.ac.uk

Abstract

Modern fact verification systems have distanced themselves from the black box paradigm by providing the evidence used to infer their veracity judgments. Hence, evidence-backed fact verification systems' performance heavily depends on the capabilities of their retrieval component to identify these facts. A popular evaluation benchmark for these systems is the FEVER task, which consists of determining the veracity of short claims using sentences extracted from Wikipedia. In this paper, we present a novel approach to the the retrieval steps of the FEVER task leveraging the graph structure of Wikipedia. The retrieval models surpass state of the art results at both sentence and document level. Additionally, we show that by feeding our retrieved evidence to the best-performing textual entailment model, we set a new state of the art in the FEVER competition.

1 Introduction

The two-year Coronavirus pandemic and the recent war in Ukraine have evidenced how easily disinformation spreads among the general public and the social consequences this can have. In the information era's day-to-day, we live in a super-connected media ecosystem that provides us with an endless stream of facts and hoaxes alike but no immediate tools to separate them (Olan et al., 2022; Barua et al., 2020). Moreover, the rapid development of larger and more capable language models has made disinformation detection significantly harder since traditional fact-verification systems, usually framed as textual entailment classification problems, are now vulnerable to synthetic disinformation attacks (Du et al., 2022; Stiff and Johansson, 2022). Therefore, modern high-performing fact-verification systems include a previous information retrieval step to condition the posterior veracity judgment on the extracted evidence (Lewis et al., 2020b; de Jong et al., 2022; Glass et al., 2022).

The FEVER task (Thorne et al., 2018a) consists in retrieving relevant evidence from Wikipedia given a claim and labeling it as either *Supports*, *Refutes*, or *Not enough info*. Traditionally, systems participating in the FEVER challenge have divided the task into three steps (Thorne et al., 2018b), each corresponding to a part of their pipeline: the document retrieval step, the sentence retrieval step, and the textual entailment step. In contrast with the last two steps, for most top-performing systems, the document retrieval module is directly inherited or slightly modified from previous work (Hanselowski et al., 2018; Nie et al., 2018). Therefore, for this step, the majority of systems follow one of these two strategies:

The MediaWiki API + span-matching system (Hanselowski et al., 2018). Filtering relevant documents by querying the MediaWiki API for each entity mentioned and discarding results if the entity is not present in the page's title.

Keyword matching + semantic similarity system (Nie et al., 2018). Keyword matching search for initial filtering and Neural Semantic Matching Model (NSMN) for scoring candidate documents using a concatenation of their title and first sentence along with the claim.

These approaches, although proven effective, pose three important limitations:

L1. The usage of MediaWiki API as a first document retrieval step limits the usability of the models outside Wikipedia's scope.

L2. The precision of representing an entire document using only its title and first sentence may prove insufficient to correctly assess semantical relevance.

L3. Discarding a document based on exact keyword matching can be excessively conser-

Proceedings of the Sixth Fact Extraction and VERification Workshop (FEVER), pages 38–48
May 5, 2023 ©2023 Association for Computational Linguistics

vative considering query-reference flexibility (e.g. *Michael Jackson-The King of Pop*).

Having identified the above research gaps, we pose the following research hypotheses:

H1. An encoder used for asymmetric semantic search eliminates the MediaWiki API dependency and can more effectively represent semantic relations between queries and documents.

H2. Considering parts of documents as a connected network of path-related pieces of information improves the retrieval quality (specially on queries requiring evidence from more than one document).

Hence, to test the above hypotheses, in this paper we present a novel approach to the document retrieval step for the FEVER task[1]; independent of external resources and capable of retrieving multi-hop evidence while handling partial and even misspelled references in claims. Although our work is mainly focused on the document retrieval step, we also provide a complementary model for sentence retrieval. Our approach establishes a new state of the art in both information retrieval steps and the textual entailment step.

2 Background

The vast majority of systems participating in the FEVER task challenge divide their pipelines into three steps and import their document retrieval step from previous work (Zhou et al., 2019; Stammbach, 2021; Krishna et al., 2022). It is worth mentioning that although some systems (Liu et al., 2020; Zhong et al., 2020; Soleimani et al., 2020) have embedded the baseline document retrieval strategies directly into their architectures, more recent models (Stammbach, 2021; Jiang et al., 2021b) have shown better results by concatenating the retrieved documents from the two baseline models (i.e., Hanselowski et al. (2018); Nie et al. (2018)) with other classical information retrieval techniques such as TF-IDF (Ramos, 2003) or BM25 (Robertson and Zaragoza, 2009).

The second step of most FEVER pipelines consists of performing sentence retrieval from the previously obtained documents. Unlike the previous step, this task has been explored from various perspectives. In the early days of the FEVER task, systems used ESIM-based architectures (Hanselowski et al., 2018; Nie et al., 2018). However, motivated by maximizing recall, the research focus changed to target the multi-hop evidence problem leading to the first iterative sentence retrieval models (Stammbach and Neumann, 2019; Subramanian and Lee, 2020). These models use transformers (Vaswani et al., 2017) to fine-tune large pre-trained language models (LM) used as backbone, such as BERT (Devlin et al., 2019), ALBERT, (Lan et al., 2020) or RoBERTa (Liu et al., 2019). Specifically, to target the multi-hop evidence problem, these models conceive the sentence retrieval step as an iterative process in which they assess the importance of new sentences by considering both the claim and the relevant sentences already retrieved.

Parallel to the iterative retrieval models, another variety of models leverage not only direct connections but the complete graph structure of Wikipedia to rank sentences (Zhong et al., 2020; Liu et al., 2020; Zhou et al., 2019) using graph neural networks (GNNs) (Scarselli et al., 2009). State-of-the-art models (Jiang et al., 2021b; Stammbach, 2021; Krishna et al., 2022) generally fall under one of these categories but have pivoted to more refined token-level representations or bigger LMs such as BigBird (Zaheer et al., 2020), T5 (Raffel et al., 2020) or DeBERTa (He et al., 2021). A recent approach, Claim-Dissector (Fajcik et al., 2022) proposes to divide the retrieved documents into blocks instead of individual sentences and encode each block individually.

The final step of the FEVER task involves recognizing textual entailment (TE). This subtask has traditionally been treated as a multi-class classification problem and tackled by fine-tuning from scratch some LM making use of transformers, alignment and concatenation of the retrieved evidence (Zhou et al., 2019; Liu et al., 2020; Subramanian and Lee, 2020). Top-performing systems in FEVER's public leaderboard (Fajcik et al., 2022; Stammbach, 2021) use DeBERTa-based models already trained over the Multi-Genre Natural Language Inference (MNLI) task (Williams et al., 2018) as backbone.

3 Formal task

The FEVER task consists in performing evidence-backed claim verification. Formally, the knowledge

[1]Results, intermediary files and code will be released on https://github.com/DanielGuzmanOlivares/fever-retrieval.

base, $\mathcal{D}$, is a collection of more than 5 million documents each corresponding to a Wikipedia page, $\mathcal{D} := \{d_i\}_i$, where each document d_i is itself a variable-size collection of sentences, $d_i := \{s^i_j\}_j$. Given the collection of documents $\mathcal{D}$ and a query (a statement) q , a valid system $\mathcal{S}$ must return a veracity assessment $\widetilde{v}$ for q along with a subset $\widetilde{\mathcal{E}}$, of at most five sentences supporting or refuting q:

$$\mathcal{S}(q;\mathcal{D}) \longrightarrow (\widetilde{v}, \widetilde{\mathcal{E}}) \quad \text{s.t.}$$

$$\begin{cases} \widetilde{\mathcal{E}} \subset \bigsqcup_{\mathcal{D}} d_i \\ |\hat{\mathcal{E}}| \leq 5 \\ \widetilde{v} \in \{\text{Supports, Refutes, Not Enough Info}\} \end{cases}$$

Datasets. The FEVER task, as of today, has three associated datasets: the training dataset, the shared task dev dataset, and the shared task test dataset (open competition) (Thorne et al., 2018b). The training dataset is the largest of the three containing 145,449 claims and is unbalanced towards the "*Supports*" class, which represents more than half of the examples. The dev and test datasets are widely used as the evaluation benchmarks for a FEVER pipeline. They are equal in size (19,998) and balanced between the three classes.

Metrics. Following previous work, for evaluating performance we use accuracy (ACC) in the textual entailment step, the FEVER score (FS)[2] for the whole pipeline, and Recall@K (R@K) for the retrieval steps. Additionally, we also consider the Mean Reciprocal Rank (MRR) and the proportion of claims where the system returns at least one relevant item (AND) in the retrieval tasks.

4 Model

Following the traditional pipeline organization, we propose a three-step architecture (see Figure 1) where: i) The document retrieval step uses partial references in the claim and document-level encoding to select an initial collection of documents that is later expanded (if necessary) for addressing the multi-hop evidence problem; ii) The sentence retrieval step combines the sentence retrieval part of $LF_{2\text{-iter}} + D_{XL}$ model (Stammbach, 2021) which is the current best-performing system with a DeBERTa-based cross-encoder (Reimers and Gurevych, 2019); iii) The textual entailment step uses the MNLI-trained DeBERTa model used in $LF_{2\text{-iter}} + D_{XL}$ with our retrieved evidence.

[2]FS is the central metric for the FEVER task. A prediction is only deemed correct if the label is correct and the evidence is sufficient.

4.1 Data processing

The whole data ecosystem associated with our proposed system is graph-based[3] and consists of:

A reference lookup table. Where all the references to documents are stored, the indexing format is (document title -> list of references) (e.g., Obama -> [Barack Obama, President Obama ...]).

A graph database. Implemented as a Neo4J database, mimics the graph structure needed to get neighbours and references from the given collection of documents.

An embedding database. Pre-computed document embeddings indexed by title to ease the workload of GPU computations.

A sentence database. Containing all the sentences for each document in the provided collection.

We implement the data interface transforming the given Wikipedia dump. This process can be summarized in the following steps for every record in the dump: i) Extract all relevant information from plain-text Wikipedia entry, this includes separated sentences, and the links to external articles; ii) The second step is querying the reference lookup table (initially empty) to check if the linked references already exist in the table. Should any of the references not be present in the table, we query the WikiMedia API to update the records; iii) Once the references are updated in the lookup table, the connections are added to the graph database as new edges; iv) The embedding database is updated with the embedding obtained from the encoder model; v) The sentence database is updated as well with the associated article sentences. This process is represented in Figure 2. In Figure 1, the data interface that the pipeline uses consists of all the aforementioned parts and is represented as *Graph-ref database*.

4.2 Document Retrieval

To the best of the authors' knowledge, the top-performing architectures use a baseline model (Hanselowski et al., 2018) approach combined with

[3]The system expects a graph of interconnected documents where connections represent references between documents.

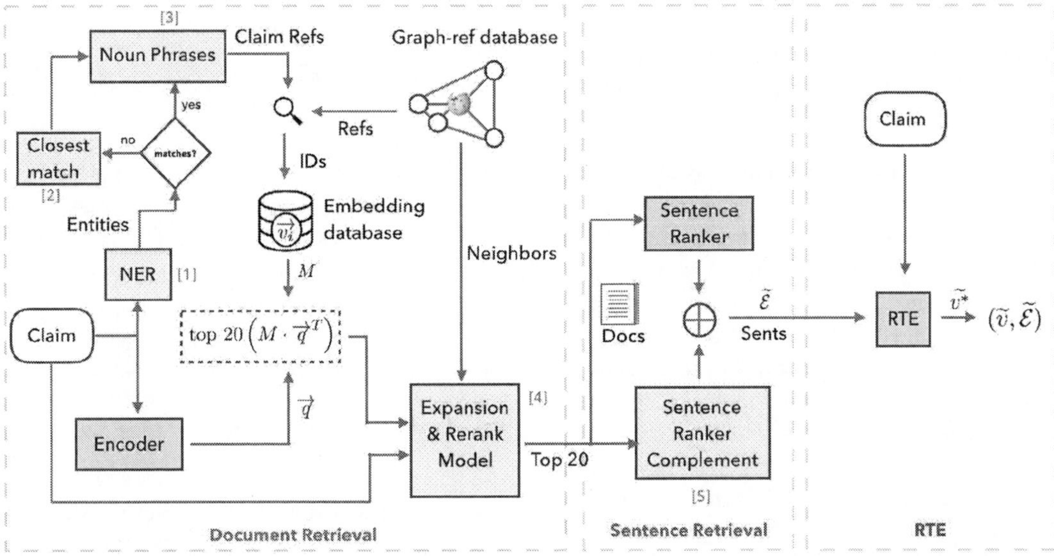

Figure 1: Full proposed pipeline. The pipeline is divided into the three traditionally used sub-architectures. The acid yellow components have been implemented from scratch for this work, whereas the salmon ones are imported from previously existing architectures. Note that each developed component has an index [x] later referenced in the corresponding module description and ablation study.

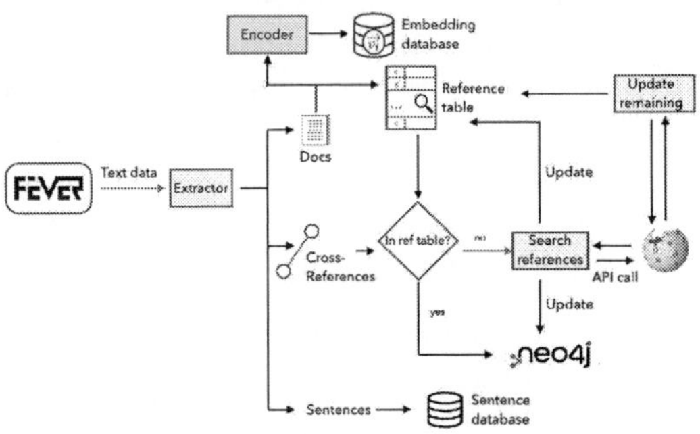

Figure 2: Data processing for the proposed solution. The green components have been implemented from scratch for this work whereas the salmon ones are imported from previously existing architectures.

TF-IDF or BM25 to return an average of 20 documents. On the other hand, the document retrieval part of our architecture consists of various modules sequentially interconnected to output a selection of document paths associated with the input query. In order, these components are the following:

Name Entity Recognition [box [1] in Figure 1]. We have trained a token-level classification module using BERT (base) as backbone, for balance between complexity and performance (F_1=0.95). Specifically, we have framed this task as a three-class classification problem (see Appendix A) using BIO labels (Ramshaw and Marcus, 1995) following the traditional approach in NER architectures (Li et al., 2020; Jiang et al., 2021a; Xia et al., 2022).

Although many existing pre-trained models exist to perform this particular task, after trying some publicly available models in random samples for NER, we found that some entities were missed. Therefore, we have opted for training our own model since a considerable number of entities in Wikipedia differ from the classical form of an entity (e.g., a country, a person, a place, a work of art). Such Wikipedia entities usually resemble something like *history of something*, *presidency of someone*, or even concepts that are not considered as entities per se like *water* or *banana*.

Closest Match [box [2] in Figure 1]. This module is motivated by observed annotation errors in the FEVER dataset (e.g., *Mellila* - *Melilla*). Since the document retrieval pipeline uses the reference lookup table for finding documents indexed by references, if one of these is not grammatically correct, it would not yield any matches. To avoid this particular case, a conditional path bifurcation has been added in between the NER module and the Noun Phrases selection (see Figure 1). In case a reference yields no results, the closest-match search triggers. The closest-match search takes as input the retrieved sequence from the NER step and finds the closest (normalized edit distance) reference to it, effectively ensuring there is always at least one associated reference for every sequence[4].

Once references have been associated to sequences of tokens, there are various plausible candidates for relevant pages. At this point, the approximate position of the entities within the claim is known thanks to the token-level classification of the NER module. However, detecting the entities' extension can be especially problematic for the cases in which an entity includes a modifier, which makes it hard for the NER system to fully recognize it as part of the relying entity. For example, in '*Charles **II** of England was born on Thursday 29 May 1630*,' the **II** directly impacts the evidence that should be retrieved.

Noun-phrases selection [box [3] in Figure 1]. This module addresses this problem by using three different language planes in order to capture entities:

The semantic plane. Uses the NER pipelines from Flair (Akbik et al., 2019) and SpaCy (Honnibal et al., 2020) since they are trained for a wider variety of entities and can retrieve information that the proposed NER system might miss.

The syntactical plane. Uses the AllenAI Open Information Extraction (OEI) system (Stanovsky et al., 2018) to extract the syntactical subject and direct object of a claim. Relevant to the cases that are not associated with an object or an event (e.g. *Water is part of the **History of Earth**.*)

The ontology plane. Rule-based parsing built on top of SpaCy's dependency parsing. Essentially retrieves modifiers not included in the entities provided by the NER module.

Finally, the information retrieved by the three planes and the already predicted references (from the NER module) are combined and later joined with the lemmatized version of the NER references (see Figure 3). This process allows us to accurately extract multiple candidate entities given a claim, mitigating the WikiMedia dependence from previously proposed solutions (see **L1** in Section 1).

Encoding. At this point, the complete set of references is available, and, by using the lookup table, the associated documents are retrieved. Since, on average, there are too many documents to move on to the next step of the FEVER pipeline, the system uses semantic relatedness to assess the importance of documents conditioned to the claim. In practice, this means encoding the claim (Hofstätter et al., 2021) to obtain the query vector $\overrightarrow{q}$. Then the vectors associated with the selected documents are retrieved from the embeddings database[5] and stacked in a matrix M. Finally, we multiply $M \cdot \overrightarrow{q}^T$ obtaining the vector of semantic closeness for every query-document pair. We select the top $\mathcal{K} = 20$ documents corresponding to the largest entries of the vector.

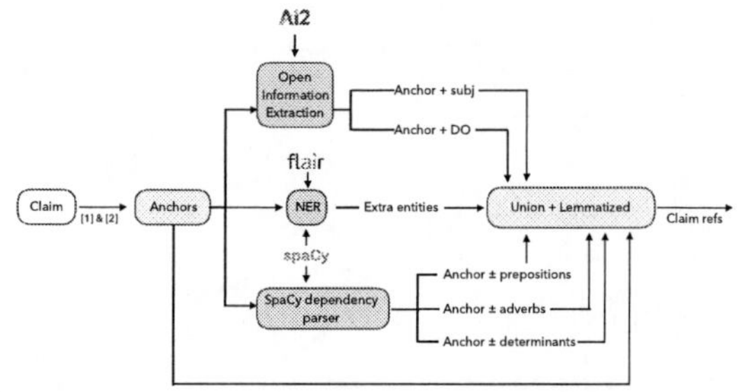

Figure 3: The Noun Phrase module internally. We use green for custom architectures and salmon for imported ones. Anchors represent the references obtained by the pipeline till this point since it obtains the probable points of the claim where entities are.

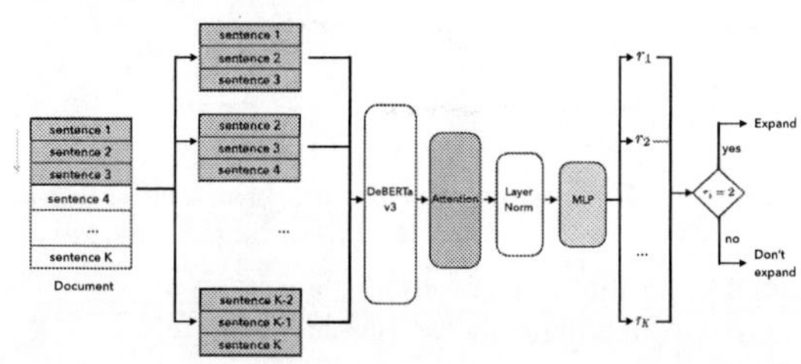

Figure 4: The Expansion model. Note the expansion window sliding (in purple).

Expansion and Rerank [box [4] in Figure 1]. This module consists of a two-step architecture that leverages the graph structure of the built database to improve recall. While the previous modules provide twenty documents directly related to the references in the claim, this module goes one step further and explores the neighbours of the provided documents (expansion) to estimate the importance of the second-order documents

[4]This makes the system more flexible than those discarding non-exact matches (see **L3** in Section 1).

[5]Note that the full documents are pre-encoded in contrast with just the title and first sentence (see **L2** in Section 1).

(neighbours) given the claim and the first-order documents.

In the expansion stage, instead of considering every neighbour of every document provided by the previous component in the pipeline, a model has been developed to decide which documents are worth expanding to optimize performance and ease the workload in the sentence retrieval step (since we only expand relevant parts of the initial document). For training this model we divide a document in consecutive overlapping (context) windows and treat the problem as a 3-way classification in which each window's class correspond to the amount of relevant information contained on it (none, some, or all) (see Appendix B).

Preliminary experiments showed that context windows of three consecutive sentences offer the best performance. For each of these, the sentences are concatenated (separated by the [SEP] special token) along with the document's title for helping coreference disambiguation (Malon, 2018). Then for every concatenation, the DeBERTa V3 model is used to obtain the context embedding from both concatenation and claim. Afterward, both embeddings are concatenated and fed to a custom attention head (see Figure 4). Finally, the document is expanded if any of the context-concatenations is evaluated as SOME INFORMATION PRESENT. Following the expansion, we group the resulting collection of documents in paths according to expansion results (i.e. for a given document d_1, if d_1 is expanded obtaining neighbours $n_1, n_2, ..., n_m$ we group paths $(d_1, n_1), (d_1, n_2), ..., (d_1, n_m)$, otherwise if $d1$ is not expanded, only (d_1) is considered as a single path).

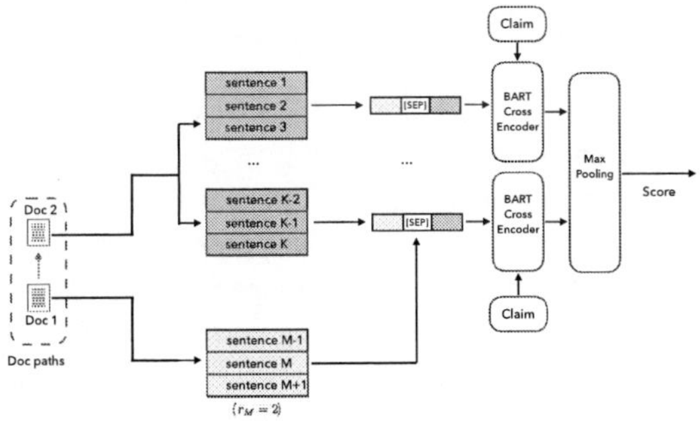

Figure 5: The Rerank model. For a case with a path of length 2, the first-order document's context window (in green) is used as a complement to every context window (sliding) for the second-order document (in purple)

Following the above module we have to assess the semantic relatedness to the query of a rather large set of interlinked documents. The Rerank model is an efficient way to accomplish this task. Internally, the model modifies the classical cross-encoder architecture to use a linked source. We can distinguish two cases regarding the input path's length:

Path of length 2. First, we start by using the context windows again, fully sliding for the second order document and just using the context window that originated the expansion in the first order document. We concatenate the sentences from the first order window with every sentence of the second order window and create a large concatenation of sentences (see Figure 5).

Path of length 1. In this case, we only have one document, so we separate every sentence from the document instead of creating concatenations.

We then feed the concatenations, along with the claim to a BART-based[6] (Lewis et al., 2020a) cross-encoder that outputs a score. We take the maximum score from all concatenations and output it as the relevance score. Finally, we sort the document paths by given score and take the maximum number of paths possible, ensuring that the total number of documents does not exceed $\mathcal{K} = 20$.

4.3 Sentence Retrieval

The sentence retrieval step of our pipeline uses a combination of the current state-of-the-art model, $LF_{2\text{-iter}} + D_{XL}$ (Stammbach, 2021), and a simple DeBERTav3-based cross-encoder combining all possible sentences from first and second order context windows for every path. For the input of both models, we use the document path collection outputted from our document retrieval pipeline. Originally, the $LF_{2\text{-iter}} + D_{XL}$ model uses UKP's (Hanselowski et al., 2018) document retrieval step combined with TF-IDF and a (query, sentence) pair evaluation based on a token-level BigBird (Zaheer et al., 2020) model for the sentence retrieval step. Particularly, the $LF_{2\text{-iter}} + D_{XL}$ sentence retrieval architecture works in two stages. On the first one, the query and all the sentences from first-order documents are evaluated and given a score. Every pair given a score greater than 0 is expanded. Finally, every expanded sentence is evaluated conditioned not only on the query but also on the first-order

[6]Preliminary tests showed that BART offered the best results among several LMs.

sentence from which it comes from (again using the BigBird model).

Although using the documents retrieved from our solution in $LF_{2\text{-iter}} + D_{XL}$ performs reasonably well on its own, we found that combining the sentence rankings from this model with the rankings from our own cross-encoder boosts global performance (see Table 4). Directly combining the rankings from both models is possible since both are based on retrieving connected (first-second order) sentences. Formally, given the definition of a ranking:

$$\widetilde{\mathcal{R}} := \{p_i\}_i$$

$$p_i = \begin{cases} (s_k^i, s_m^j), & \text{if } d_j \text{ expanded from } d_i. \\ (s_k^i) & \text{if } d_i \text{ has no expansion.} \end{cases}$$

We can define the *order* of p_i, a path in ranking $\widetilde{\mathcal{R}}$, as

$$\varphi_{\widetilde{\mathcal{R}}}(p_i) = \begin{cases} i & \text{if } p_i \subset \widetilde{\mathcal{R}} \\ 0 & \text{otherwise} \end{cases}$$

In this context, the combination of the rankings $\widetilde{\mathcal{R}}_{LF}$ and $\widetilde{\mathcal{R}}_{CE}$ corresponding to the $LF_{2\text{-iter}} + D_{XL}$ system and our cross encoder respectively, is defined as:

$$\widetilde{\mathcal{E}} = \underset{A \subset \widetilde{\mathcal{R}}_{LF} \cup \widetilde{\mathcal{R}}_{CE}}{\operatorname{argmax}} \sum_A \varphi_{\widetilde{\mathcal{R}}_{CE}}(p) + \varphi_{\widetilde{\mathcal{R}}_{LF}}(p) \quad \text{s.t.}$$

$$\sum_A |p| \leq 5$$

5 Experimental Evaluation and Results

We present our results for the development dataset at every stage and the FEVER challenge competition (test set) results:

Document retrieval. As previously commented, some of the most recent approaches add the documents retrieved from classic techniques such as TF-IDF and BM25 to the results retrieved from their main document retrieval architectures. In doing so, the retrieved documents lose the ranking order, and it would be inaccurate to directly compare recall@K since the results from these combined systems are not rankings but rather collections of documents. Therefore, we compare our results with the unaltered baseline systems in Table 1 and establish a new state of the art for this stage, surpassing UKP's results by 3.07%. A comparison of our approach's performance varying the number of documents can be found in Table 2. We observe a high and steady MRR metric, which means that in most cases, there is a relevant document within the top 5 documents. Hence, most of the recall errors are likely claims that are not correctly interpreted (i.e., no relevant document in all ranking) or multi-hop evidence cases in which not all the evidence was retrieved. Finally, we perform an ablation study regarding all the modules in the document retrieval step of our solution (see Table 3), from which it can be inferred that the Noun Phrases (box [3] in Figure 1) and the Expansion & Rerank (box [4] in Figure 1) modules are the parts that have a higher impact on performance. Additionally, it is worth noting that the Closest Match module (box [2] in Figure 1) does not have a significant impact on general performance, meaning that although some examples exist, there are not many instances with grammatical errors within the FEVER dev dataset.

System	R@10
UKP (Hanselowski et al., 2018)	93.55
UNC (Nie et al., 2018)	92.82
Ours	**96.62**

Table 1: Comparison of document retrieval system's recall with existing architectures

Nº Docs	Recall	AND	MRR
5	95.54	97.26	0.935
10	96.62	97.96	0.935
15	97.08	98.20	0.935
20	97.20	98.29	0.935

Table 2: Document retrieval metrics of our proposed solution considering different number of documents.

Sentence retrieval. In Table 4, we report the results with and without combining the $LF_{2\text{-iter}} + D_{XL}$ system to our cross-encoder for this stage, along with a performance comparison with the existing architectures. Our proposed solution outperforms the current state of the art by 1.05 %. Note that $LF_{2\text{-iter}} + D_{XL}$ system also surpasses the state of the art when given the documents selected from our document retrieval step. Indicating that our document retrieval strategy potentially improves the effectiveness of a sentence retrieval module.

Textual entailment. In the test set (competition),

Combination	R@20
[1]	94.50
[1] + [2]	94.74
[1] + [3]	95.03
[1] + [2] + [3]	95.27
[1] + [4]	95.30
[1] + [2] + [4]	95.80
[1] + [3] + [4]	97.01
[1] + [2] + [3] + [4]	97.20

Table 3: Ablation study for the proposed system. Note that every component is referred to as an index [x] which is depicted in Figure 1.

	System	R@5	Acc	FS
Development dataset	(Hanselowski et al., 2018)	86.02	68.49	64.74
	(Nie et al., 2018)	86.79	69.72	66.49
	(Subramanian and Lee, 2020)	90.50	75.77	73.44
	(Stammbach and Neumann, 2019)	89.80	72.10	-
	(Zhou et al., 2019)	86.72	74.84	70.69
	(Liu et al., 2020)†	94.37	78.29	76.11
	(Zhong et al., 2020)	90.50	79.16	-
	(Jiang et al., 2021b)	90.54	**81.26**	77.75
	(Krishna et al., 2022)	-	80.74	79.07
	(Stammbach, 2021)	93.62	-	-
	(Chen et al., 2022)	79.61	79.44	77.38
	(Fajcik et al., 2022)	93.30	80.80	78.00
	Ours [1-4]	93.93	80.03	78.36
	Ours [1-5] (Full)	**94.67**	80.95	**79.12**
Test dataset	(Zhou et al., 2019)	-	71.60	67.10
	(Liu et al., 2020)	-	74.07	70.38
	(Zhong et al., 2020)	-	74.64	71.48
	(Jiang et al., 2021b)	-	79.35	75.87
	(Krishna et al., 2022)	-	79.47	76.82
	(Stammbach, 2021)	-	79.16	76.68
	(Chen et al., 2022)	-	75.24	71.17
	(Fajcik et al., 2022)	-	79.27	76.45
	(Izacard et al., 2022)‡	-	**80.06**	21.29
	Ours[1-5] (Full)	-	79.69	**76.91**

Table 4: Performance for the second and third stages in the development and test datasets. † The system uses gold evidence when reporting these results. ‡ The system was not specifically designed for FEVER, trained with the whole Wikipedia for performing fact verification, hence the disparity in Acc and FS.

regarding the Fever Score, our proposal achieves a new state of the art by using our retrieved evidence with the approach followed in $LF_{2\text{-iter}} + D_{XL}$. Additionally, we report the second-highest accuracy score, 79.69%, only surpassed by the Atlas system (Izacard et al., 2022). In the development dataset, we report a competitive 80.95% accuracy while our Fever Score (FS), 79.12%, outperforms the current state of the art.

6 Conclusions

In this paper, we have proposed a retrieval architecture that combined with a textual entailment model outperforms the state of the art in all stages of the FEVER task. Our architecture starts by leveraging document-level semantic representation to narrow an initial collection of documents to 20 candidates. Filtered results are later expanded using the graph structure inherent to the built database. Once expansion is completed, our model scores the context windows inside documents, ranks the link paths, and takes the top elements from the ranking, ensuring that no more than 20 documents are retrieved. Then, the documents are passed on to the sentence retrieval model that combines the prediction of the $LF_{2\text{-iter}} + D_{XL}$ system with a simple cross-encoder to obtain a sentence-paths ranking. Finally, following the approach in $LF_{2\text{-iter}} + D_{XL}$, a pre-trained DeBERTa-based MNLI model is used and later post-processed based on the output logits.

Regarding our initial research hypotheses; considering the results obtained in the ablation study (see Table 3) and the sentence retrieval steps (see Table 1, Table 4) we can conclude that: i) We can use semantic encoding as an alternative to keyword matching to build a retrieval system independent of external resources (**H1**); ii) Expanding and reranking connected paths of information using small context windows inside documents improve retrieval quality (**H2**).

Limitations

The main limitation of our model concerns the expansion operation in the retrieval steps. In particular the system assumes a constant maximum length of two hops. This decision leads to some recall errors, however, in the FEVER development dataset, more than 99% of the evidence can be retrieved with at most two sentences. Another limitation of our model is relying on a cascade-based architecture i.e., the performance of one step is always bounded by the performance on the previous step. Additionally, although not directly dependent on external resources, we expect a graph structure between documents for the model to work and this could prove complicated to manage depending on environments different than Wikipedia.

Ethics Statement

The presented work could help to more accurately extract information to verify statements. However, the system relies on contrasting facts using a "truth" database. The existence of such a resource is not a trivial assumption to make, especially if we consider open sources of information such as social networks in which virtually anyone can add content. Consequently, and in addition to the fact that no system is perfect, we discourage the usage of our work as any kind of ground truth for any fact verification task if the reference database cannot be checked by experts both in terms of accuracy and possible biases.

Acknowledgements

We sincerely thank the anonymous reviewers for their thorough reviewing and valuable suggestions. The research of Guzman-Olivares and Quijano-Sanchez was conducted with financial support from the Spanish Ministry of Science and Innovation, grant PID2019-108965GB-I00. The research of Liberatore was partially funded by the grant PID2019-108679RB-I00 of the Spanish Ministry of Science and Innovation.

References

Alan Akbik, Tanja Bergmann, Duncan Blythe, Kashif Rasul, Stefan Schweter, and Roland Vollgraf. 2019. FLAIR: An easy-to-use framework for state-of-the-art NLP. In *NAACL 2019, 2019 Annual Conference of the North American Chapter of the Association for Computational Linguistics (Demonstrations)*, pages 54–59.

Zapan Barua, Sajib Barua, Salma Aktar, Najma Kabir, and Mingze Li. 2020. Effects of misinformation on covid-19 individual responses and recommendations for resilience of disastrous consequences of misinformation. *Progress in Disaster Science*, 8:100119.

Jiangui Chen, Ruqing Zhang, Jiafeng Guo, Yixing Fan, and Xueqi Cheng. 2022. Gere: Generative evidence retrieval for fact verification. In *Proceedings of the 45th International ACM SIGIR Conference on Research and Development in Information Retrieval*, SIGIR '22, page 2184–2189, New York, NY, USA. Association for Computing Machinery.

Michiel de Jong, Yury Zemlyanskiy, Nicholas FitzGerald, Fei Sha, and William W. Cohen. 2022. Mention memory: incorporating textual knowledge into transformers through entity mention attention. In *International Conference on Learning Representations*.

Jacob Devlin, Ming-Wei Chang, Kenton Lee, and Kristina Toutanova. 2019. BERT: Pre-training of deep bidirectional transformers for language understanding. In *Proceedings of the 2019 Conference of the North American Chapter of the Association for Computational Linguistics: Human Language Technologies, Volume 1 (Long and Short Papers)*, pages 4171–4186, Minneapolis, Minnesota. Association for Computational Linguistics.

Yibing Du, Antoine Bosselut, and Christopher D. Manning. 2022. Synthetic disinformation attacks on automated fact verification systems. *Proceedings of the AAAI Conference on Artificial Intelligence*, 36(10):10581–10589.

Martin Fajcik, Petr Motlécek, and Pavel Smrz. 2022. Claim-dissector: An interpretable fact-checking system with joint re-ranking and veracity prediction. *CoRR*, abs/2207.14116v1.

Michael Glass, Gaetano Rossiello, Md Faisal Mahbub Chowdhury, Ankita Naik, Pengshan Cai, and Alfio Gliozzo. 2022. Re2G: Retrieve, rerank, generate. In *Proceedings of the 2022 Conference of the North American Chapter of the Association for Computational Linguistics: Human Language Technologies*, pages 2701–2715, Seattle, United States. Association for Computational Linguistics.

Andreas Hanselowski, Hao Zhang, Zile Li, Daniil Sorokin, Benjamin Schiller, Claudia Schulz, and Iryna Gurevych. 2018. UKP-athene: Multi-sentence textual entailment for claim verification. In *Proceedings of the First Workshop on Fact Extraction and VERification (FEVER)*, pages 103–108, Brussels, Belgium. Association for Computational Linguistics.

Pengcheng He, Jianfeng Gao, and Weizhu Chen. 2021. Debertav3: Improving deberta using electra-style pre-training with gradient-disentangled embedding sharing.

Sebastian Hofstätter, Sheng-Chieh Lin, Jheng-Hong Yang, Jimmy Lin, and Allan Hanbury. 2021. Efficiently teaching an effective dense retriever with balanced topic aware sampling. In *Proceedings of the 44th International ACM SIGIR Conference on Research and Development in Information Retrieval*, SIGIR '21, page 113–122, New York, NY, USA. Association for Computing Machinery.

Matthew Honnibal, Ines Montani, Sofie Van Landeghem, and Adriane Boyd. 2020. spaCy: Industrial-strength Natural Language Processing in Python.

Gautier Izacard, Patrick Lewis, Maria Lomeli, Lucas Hosseini, Fabio Petroni, Timo Schick, Jane Dwivedi-Yu, Armand Joulin, Sebastian Riedel, and Edouard

Grave. 2022. Few-shot learning with retrieval augmented language models.

Haoming Jiang, Danqing Zhang, Tianyu Cao, Bing Yin, and Tuo Zhao. 2021a. Named entity recognition with small strongly labeled and large weakly labeled data. In *Proceedings of the 59th Annual Meeting of the Association for Computational Linguistics and the 11th International Joint Conference on Natural Language Processing (Volume 1: Long Papers)*, pages 1775–1789, Online. Association for Computational Linguistics.

Kelvin Jiang, Ronak Pradeep, and Jimmy Lin. 2021b. Exploring listwise evidence reasoning with t5 for fact verification. In *Proceedings of the 59th Annual Meeting of the Association for Computational Linguistics and the 11th International Joint Conference on Natural Language Processing (Volume 2: Short Papers)*, pages 402–410, Online. Association for Computational Linguistics.

Amrith Krishna, Sebastian Riedel, and Andreas Vlachos. 2022. ProoFVer: Natural logic theorem proving for fact verification. *Transactions of the Association for Computational Linguistics*, 10:1013–1030.

Zhenzhong Lan, Mingda Chen, Sebastian Goodman, Kevin Gimpel, Piyush Sharma, and Radu Soricut. 2020. ALBERT: A lite BERT for self-supervised learning of language representations. In *8th International Conference on Learning Representations, ICLR 2020, Addis Ababa, Ethiopia, April 26-30, 2020*. OpenReview.net.

Mike Lewis, Yinhan Liu, Naman Goyal, Marjan Ghazvininejad, Abdelrahman Mohamed, Omer Levy, Veselin Stoyanov, and Luke Zettlemoyer. 2020a. BART: Denoising sequence-to-sequence pre-training for natural language generation, translation, and comprehension. In *Proceedings of the 58th Annual Meeting of the Association for Computational Linguistics*, pages 7871–7880, Online. Association for Computational Linguistics.

Patrick S. H. Lewis, Ethan Perez, Aleksandra Piktus, Fabio Petroni, Vladimir Karpukhin, Naman Goyal, Heinrich Küttler, Mike Lewis, Wen-tau Yih, Tim Rocktäschel, Sebastian Riedel, and Douwe Kiela. 2020b. Retrieval-augmented generation for knowledge-intensive NLP tasks. In *Advances in Neural Information Processing Systems 33: Annual Conference on Neural Information Processing Systems 2020, NeurIPS 2020, December 6-12, 2020, virtual*.

Jing Li, Aixin Sun, Ray Han, and Chenliang Li. 2020. A survey on deep learning for named entity recognition. *IEEE Transactions on Knowledge and Data Engineering*, PP:1–1.

Yinhan Liu, Myle Ott, Naman Goyal, Jingfei Du, Mandar Joshi, Danqi Chen, Omer Levy, Mike Lewis, Luke Zettlemoyer, and Veselin Stoyanov. 2019. Roberta: A robustly optimized bert pretraining approach.

Zhenghao Liu, Chenyan Xiong, Maosong Sun, and Zhiyuan Liu. 2020. Fine-grained fact verification with kernel graph attention network. In *Proceedings of the 58th Annual Meeting of the Association for Computational Linguistics*, pages 7342–7351, Online. Association for Computational Linguistics.

Christopher Malon. 2018. Team papelo: Transformer networks at FEVER. In *Proceedings of the First Workshop on Fact Extraction and VERification (FEVER)*, pages 109–113, Brussels, Belgium. Association for Computational Linguistics.

Yixin Nie, Haonan Chen, and Mohit Bansal. 2018. Combining fact extraction and verification with neural semantic matching networks.

Femi Olan, Uchitha Jayawickrama, Emmanuel Ogiemwonyi Arakpogun, Jana Suklan, and Shaofeng Liu. 2022. Fake news on social media: the impact on society. *Information Systems Frontiers*.

Colin Raffel, Noam Shazeer, Adam Roberts, Katherine Lee, Sharan Narang, Michael Matena, Yanqi Zhou, Wei Li, and Peter J. Liu. 2020. Exploring the limits of transfer learning with a unified text-to-text transformer. *Journal of Machine Learning Research*, 21(140):1–67.

Juan Ramos. 2003. Using tf-idf to determine word relevance in document queries.

Lance Ramshaw and Mitch Marcus. 1995. Text chunking using transformation-based learning. In *Third Workshop on Very Large Corpora*.

Nils Reimers and Iryna Gurevych. 2019. Sentence-BERT: Sentence embeddings using Siamese BERT-networks. In *Proceedings of the 2019 Conference on Empirical Methods in Natural Language Processing and the 9th International Joint Conference on Natural Language Processing (EMNLP-IJCNLP)*, pages 3982–3992, Hong Kong, China. Association for Computational Linguistics.

Stephen Robertson and Hugo Zaragoza. 2009. The probabilistic relevance framework: Bm25 and beyond. *Foundations and Trends in Information Retrieval*, 3:333–389.

Franco Scarselli, Marco Gori, Ah Chung Tsoi, Markus Hagenbuchner, and Gabriele Monfardini. 2009. The graph neural network model. *IEEE Transactions on Neural Networks*, 20(1):61–80.

Amir Soleimani, Christof Monz, and Marcel Worring. 2020. Bert for evidence retrieval and claim verification. In *Advances in Information Retrieval*, pages 359–366, Cham. Springer International Publishing.

Dominik Stammbach. 2021. Evidence selection as a token-level prediction task. In *Proceedings of the Fourth Workshop on Fact Extraction and VERification (FEVER)*, pages 14–20, Dominican Republic. Association for Computational Linguistics.

Dominik Stammbach and Guenter Neumann. 2019. Team DOMLIN: Exploiting evidence enhancement for the FEVER shared task. In *Proceedings of the Second Workshop on Fact Extraction and VERification (FEVER)*, pages 105–109, Hong Kong, China. Association for Computational Linguistics.

Gabriel Stanovsky, Julian Michael, Luke Zettlemoyer, and I. Dagan. 2018. Supervised open information extraction. In *NAACL-HLT*.

Harald Stiff and Fredrik Johansson. 2022. Detecting computer-generated disinformation. *International Journal of Data Science and Analytics*, 13(4):363–383.

Shyam Subramanian and Kyumin Lee. 2020. Hierarchical Evidence Set Modeling for automated fact extraction and verification. In *Proceedings of the 2020 Conference on Empirical Methods in Natural Language Processing (EMNLP)*, pages 7798–7809, Online. Association for Computational Linguistics.

James Thorne, Andreas Vlachos, Christos Christodoulopoulos, and Arpit Mittal. 2018a. FEVER: a large-scale dataset for fact extraction and VERification. In *Proceedings of the 2018 Conference of the North American Chapter of the Association for Computational Linguistics: Human Language Technologies, Volume 1 (Long Papers)*, pages 809–819, New Orleans, Louisiana. Association for Computational Linguistics.

James Thorne, Andreas Vlachos, Oana Cocarascu, Christos Christodoulopoulos, and Arpit Mittal. 2018b. The fact extraction and VERification (FEVER) shared task. In *Proceedings of the First Workshop on Fact Extraction and VERification (FEVER)*, pages 1–9, Brussels, Belgium. Association for Computational Linguistics.

Ashish Vaswani, Noam Shazeer, Niki Parmar, Jakob Uszkoreit, Llion Jones, Aidan N Gomez, Ł ukasz Kaiser, and Illia Polosukhin. 2017. Attention is all you need. In *Advances in Neural Information Processing Systems*, volume 30. Curran Associates, Inc.

Adina Williams, Nikita Nangia, and Samuel Bowman. 2018. A broad-coverage challenge corpus for sentence understanding through inference. In *Proceedings of the 2018 Conference of the North American Chapter of the Association for Computational Linguistics: Human Language Technologies, Volume 1 (Long Papers)*, pages 1112–1122, New Orleans, Louisiana. Association for Computational Linguistics.

Yu Xia, Quan Wang, Yajuan Lyu, Yong Zhu, Wenhao Wu, Sujian Li, and Dai Dai. 2022. Learn and review: Enhancing continual named entity recognition via reviewing synthetic samples. In *Findings of the Association for Computational Linguistics: ACL 2022*, pages 2291–2300, Dublin, Ireland. Association for Computational Linguistics.

Manzil Zaheer, Guru Guruganesh, Kumar Avinava Dubey, Joshua Ainslie, Chris Alberti, Santiago Ontanon, Philip Pham, Anirudh Ravula, Qifan Wang, Li Yang, and Amr Ahmed. 2020. Big bird: Transformers for longer sequences. In *Advances in Neural Information Processing Systems*, volume 33, pages 17283–17297. Curran Associates, Inc.

Wanjun Zhong, Jingjing Xu, Duyu Tang, Zenan Xu, Nan Duan, Ming Zhou, Jiahai Wang, and Jian Yin. 2020. Reasoning over semantic-level graph for fact checking. In *Proceedings of the 58th Annual Meeting of the Association for Computational Linguistics*, pages 6170–6180, Online. Association for Computational Linguistics.

Jie Zhou, Xu Han, Cheng Yang, Zhiyuan Liu, Lifeng Wang, Changcheng Li, and Maosong Sun. 2019. GEAR: Graph-based evidence aggregating and reasoning for fact verification. In *Proceedings of the 57th Annual Meeting of the Association for Computational Linguistics*, pages 892–901, Florence, Italy. Association for Computational Linguistics.

A Synthetic NER Dataset

The synthetic dataset for the NER problem has been built as follows: i) Given a claim, separate it by words and extract the associated pages from the gold evidence; ii) Use edit distance at token level to perform keyword matching with the previously separated words; iii) Discard the matchings having an edit distance smaller than a threshold (we used .4); iv) Use a BERT-based tokenizer to separate the sentence. For each matched sequence, label the first belonging token as B (begin) and every other as I (intermediary); v) Any token that is not either I or B is labeled as O (Null).

B Synthetic Rerank Dataset

The rank dataset has been built as follows: i) Divide the claims into two groups regarding the number of evidence pieces (one or two) needed for the veracity judgment to be valid; ii) Balance the groups by under-sampling the group with only one piece of evidence needed; iii) Join the groups and randomly create sequences of context windows from first and second-order documents; iv) Give these sequences a score according to the information they present regarding information completeness: 0 for unrelated content, 0.5 for related but incomplete (second-order case in which only one of the context windows is correct), and 1 for complete evidence.

"World Knowledge" in Multiple Choice Reading Comprehension

Adian Liusie* ALTA Institute, Cambridge University al826@cam.ac.uk

Vatsal Raina* ALTA Institute, Cambridge University vr311@cam.ac.uk

Mark Gales ALTA Institute, Cambridge University mjfg@cam.ac.uk

Abstract

Recently it has been shown that without any access to the contextual passage, multiple choice reading comprehension (MCRC) systems are able to answer questions significantly better than random on average. These systems use their accumulated "world knowledge" to directly answer questions, rather than using information from the passage. This paper examines the possibility of exploiting this observation as a tool for test designers to ensure that the form of "world knowledge" is acceptable for a particular set of questions. We propose information-theory based metrics that enable the level of "world knowledge" exploited by systems to be assessed. Two metrics are described: the expected number of options, which measures whether a passage-free system can identify the answer to a question using world knowledge; and the contextual mutual information, which measures the importance of context for a given question. We demonstrate that questions with low expected number of options, and hence answerable by the shortcut system, are often similarly answerable by humans without context. This highlights that the general knowledge 'shortcuts' could be equally used by exam candidates, and that our proposed metrics may be helpful for future test designers to monitor the quality of questions.

1 Introduction

Reading comprehension (RC) exams are used extensively in a wide range of language competency examinations (Alderson, 2000), and have become a ubiquitous assessment method to probe how well candidates can read a passage and understand the text's core meaning. A fundamental assumption of RC exams is that to answer any of the questions correctly, one has to read the passage, comprehend its meaning, and identify the relevant information of a given question. However, recent work has shown that multiple-choice machine reading comprehension (MCMRC) systems without access to the passage can achieve reasonable performance (Pang et al., 2022), showing that the models may be doing less comprehension than anticipated.

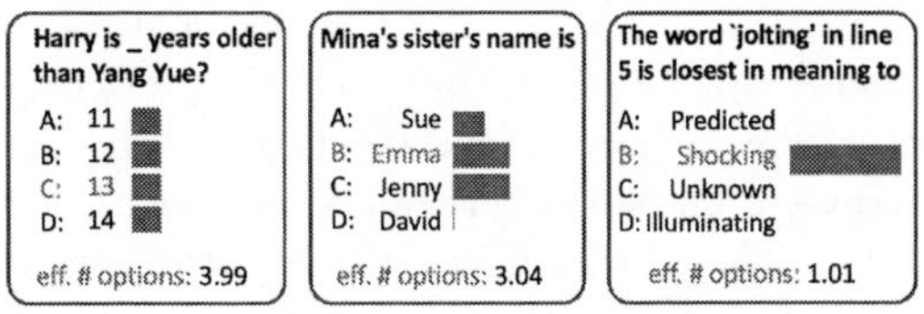

Figure 1: Output probabilities of our model (trained with contexts omitted) on real RACE++ (Liang et al., 2019) examples. 'Effective number of options' is a metric that captures the model's confidence.

In this paper we analyse this phenomena and for several standard MCMRC datasets (Liang et al., 2019; Huang et al., 2019; Yu et al., 2020) verify that passage-free baselines are able to achieve performance significantly better than random. We show that a subset of questions can be answered accurately and confidently without access to the contextual passage, where further analysis shows this is partly due to the presence of low-quality distractors, i.e. options that can be eliminated using only the question. As an example, given the question "Mina's sister's name is:", one can eliminate any options that use a traditionally male name (see Figure 1). This highlights a potential 'shortcut' candidates could use to answer questions while bypassing the context. Our work raises awareness to this potential flaw, and proposes a simple solution to catch questions that can be answered without comprehension. The proposed metrics might be a useful tool for future multiple-choice RC test designers to ensure that all questions truly assess

*Equal Contribution

Proceedings of the Sixth Fact Extraction and VERification Workshop (FEVER), pages 49–57
May 5, 2023 ©2023 Association for Computational Linguistics

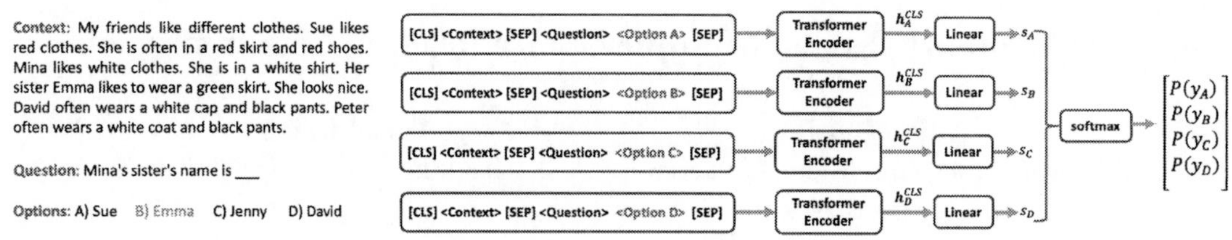

Figure 2: Model architecture.

reading comprehension ability.

Machine reading comprehension (MRC) is a highly researched area, with state-of-the-art (SoTA) systems (Zhang et al., 2021; Yamada et al., 2020; Zaheer et al., 2020; Wang et al., 2022) often approaching or even exceeding human level performance on public benchmarking leaderboards (Clark et al., 2018; Lai et al., 2017; Trischler et al., 2017; Yang et al., 2018). Existing work has analysed the robustness of MRC systems, where researchers have questioned whether systems fully leverage context and whether they accomplish the underlying comprehension task (Sugawara et al., 2020; Rajpurkar et al., 2016; Kaushik and Lipton, 2018; Jia and Liang, 2017; Si et al., 2019). Most notably Kaushik and Lipton (2018) show that for a range of question-answering tasks, passage-only systems can often achieve remarkable performance, which has been observed in the MCRC setting (Pang et al., 2022).

Most existing work has discussed model robustness, demonstrating that for some tasks it is possible to obtain high average system performance with no context information. In contrast, this paper focuses on the attributes of individual questions and options, identifying questions where "world knowledge" can be leveraged, and the extent to which this knowledge can be leveraged. This could be a useful tool to enable test designers to monitor the questions being proposed, and whether alternative distractors or questions should be considered.

2 Multiple choice reading comprehension

Multiple-choice reading comprehension is a popular task where given a context passage C and question Q, the correct answer must be deduced from a set of answer options $\{O\}$. Current SoTA MRC systems are dominated by pre-trained language models (PrLMs) based on the transformer encoder architecture (Devlin et al., 2019; Liu et al., 2019; Clark et al., 2020).

Model Architecture Our question-answering system follows the standard MCMRC architecture of Figure 2 (Yu et al., 2020; Raina and Gales, 2022). Each option is individually encoded along with the question and the context into a score, and a softmax layer converts the 4 options' scores into a probability distribution. At inference, the predicted answer is the option with the greatest probability.

'No Context' Shortcut System A requirement for good MCRC questions is that information from both the question and the context passage must be used to determine the correct answer. To probe whether this is an issue for MCMRC, we train systems using 'context free' inputs (similar to Pang et al. (2022)). The standard set-up (Figure 2) is still followed, however the input is now altered to exclude the context, as shown in Figure 3.

Standard	Q+{O}+C	[CLS] <Context> [SEP] <Question> <Option> [SEP]
Context-free	Q+{O}	[CLS] <Question> <Option> [SEP]

Figure 3: System inputs for shortcut system.

Effective Number of Options Consider the output probability distribution of the predicted answer, $\text{P}(y)$. One can determine the entropy, $\mathcal{H}(Y)$, which can be converted into the more interpretable *effective number of options*, $\mathcal{N}(Y)$, a value bounded between 1 and the maximum number of options:

$$\mathcal{N}(Y) = 2^{\mathcal{H}(Y)}, \ \ \mathcal{H}(Y) = -\sum_{y \in Y} \text{P}(y) \log_2 \text{P}(y) \quad (1)$$

For well designed questions, one would expect systems with missing information (i.e. the 'shortcut' models) to have no information of what the answer is. This would correspond to a uniform distribution output (the distribution of maximum entropy), with an effective number of options equal to the total number of answer options. However, if the effective number of options is significantly lower than the total number of answer options, then this implies that prior information stored during training can be used to answer the question, without comprehension.

Mutual Information To probe how much information is gained by the context, one can additionally look at an approximation of mutual information of the context. This looks at how much the entropy decreases between the 'no context' shortcut system and the 'context' baseline system .

$$\mathcal{I}(Y;C|Q,\{O\}) = \mathcal{H}(Y|Q,\{O\}) - \mathcal{H}(Y|Q,\{O\},C) \quad (2)$$

An alternative approach would be to use random contexts (Creswell and Shanahan, 2022) however we consider the stricter 'no context' setting.

3 Experiments

Data We consider three popular MCMRC datasets: RACE++ (Lai et al., 2017), COSMOSQA (Huang et al., 2019) and ReClor (Yu et al., 2020). RACE++ is a dataset of English comprehension questions for Chinese high school students, COSMOSQA is a large scale commonsense-based reading comprehension dataset, while ReClor is a challenging logical reasoning dataset at a graduate student level. All datasets have 4 options per question, one of which being the correct answer.

	TRN	DEV	EVL
RACE++	100,388	5,599	5,642
COSMOS	25,262	2,985	–
ReClor	4,638	500	1000

Table 1: Dataset statistics

Training An ELECTRA-large[1] model is fine-tuned on the training split `TRN`, hyper-parameters are tuned on the developement set `DEV`, and performance reported on the test split `EVL` for RACE++ (`DEV` splits are used for COSMOS and ReClor due to unavailability of the `EVL` splits). All model parameters (transformer and classifier) are updated during fine-tuning. Additionally, models are trained and evaluated using the 'no context', as described in Section 2. Final hyperparameters are given in Appendix B.1. Three seeds are trained, and ensemble accuracy is used as the default metric when reporting performance.[2]

[1]https://huggingface.co/docs/transformers/model_doc/electra

[2]code for experiments available at: https://github.com/adianliusie/MCRC

3.1 Results

Context-Free Performance We compare the performance of the baseline 'standard' system against the shortcut 'no context' systems for the various MCMRC datasets. Table 2 illustrates that the shortcut systems achieve high performance across all MCMRC datasets, all above 50%, significantly above the expected random performance of 25%. Further, we find that the shortcut rules can generalise across domains, most notably seen with the 54% performance when training the shortcut system on RACE and evaluating on COSMOS. This highlights that the shortcut performance cannot be explained purely by dataset bias, but that there is a skill, unrelated to comprehension, that the systems are meaningfully leveraging.

Training data		RACE++	COSMOS	ReClor
	–	25.00	25.00	25.00
RACE++	stan.	**85.01**	70.05	48.60
	no con.	**57.32**	54.04	34.80
COSMOS	stan.	66.81	**84.49**	41.20
	no con.	38.73	**68.51**	27.80
ReClor	stan.	52.69	41.68	**69.80**
	no con.	31.27	33.13	**51.80**

Table 2: Cross-performance of systems on RACE++, COSMOSQA and ReClor (standard vs no context).

RACE++ Effective Number of Options Figure 4 presents the count and accuracy plots of the effective number of options (bin width of 0.2) for both the standard and shortcut systems on RACE++ (see Appendix for other datasets). The counts plot show the number of questions within the bin range, while accuracy refers to the accuracy over all the examples within the bin. Since the systems are slightly overconfident[3], the systems' output probabilities are calibrated using temperature annealing (Guo et al., 2017) (see Appendix B.3).

The baseline system has high certainty for most points, which is somewhat expected given the baseline's high accuracy. However the shortcut system, without any contextual information, has a significant number of examples in the very low entropy region. This shows that for a subset of questions, the system can confidently answer questions correctly without doing any comprehension at all. In other cases, the shortcut system can leverage some information from the

[3]For both models, the mean of the maximum probability is 5% above the overall accuracy.

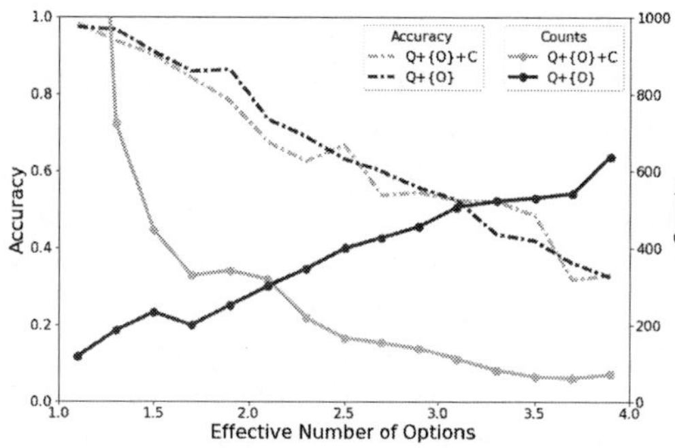

Figure 4: Distribution of effective number of options and corresponding (binned) accuracy.

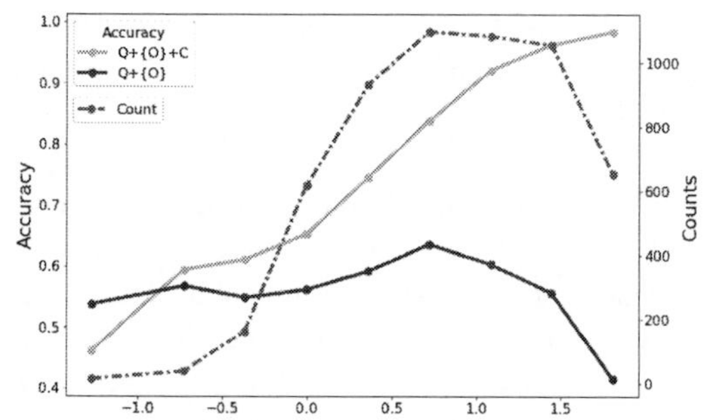

Figure 5: Distribution of counts and corresponding accuracy when points are sorted by MI approximation.

question and can reduce the number of effective options to between 2-3, which implies that certain poor distractors can be eliminated by the question alone. We also show that for both models, there is a clear linear relationship between uncertainty and accuracy, illustrating that the context-free system's use of world knowledge is sensible and that it leverages meaningful task information (see Appendix D for low-entropy examples). This confirms that the systems are well calibrated and that the effective number of options is a good measure of actual model uncertainty.

Mutual Information To further look at the influence of context, the mutual information (MI) between prediction and context was approximated for each example using Equation 2. Examples with a high MI are questions where the model is certain of the answer with context, but is uncertain without context - a desired property for comprehension questions. Figure 5 shows the counts when all the examples are ordered by MI (see Equation 2) along with both the baseline and shortcut system accuracies. We note that the count distribution has a mix of high and low MI questions, which shows that the benefit of context is not a system-wide property but instead varies over questions. The accuracy of the baseline system increases considerably when context is useful, while accuracy falls for the shortcut system. It is interesting that a small fraction of questions have negative MI. Though MI should always be positive, negative values can be observed since models are only approximations of the true underlying distributions. The low accuracy of the shortcut model on negative MI questions occurs when standard world knowledge is not consistent with the information in the context.

Human Evaluation of Metrics We perform human evaluation to judge the practical use of our metrics. We select 100 questions with lowest and highest entropy, and three volunteer graduate students independently answer the questions without access to the context. We further select 50 questions with lowest and highest MI, and get our volunteers to first answer questions without context, then with context, and calculate the accuracy increase. All questions are shuffled, and volunteers attempt to best answer all questions. We find that our metrics are very effective in measuring their desired properties. Without context, humans are often able to answer the questions that the shortcut systems answer confidently, with humans achieving an average accuracy of 92% on the 100 lowest entropy and 32% on the 100 highest entropy examples respectively. Further, for high MI questions humans get a performance boost of 71% when context is provided, and only 22% for low mutual information questions.

	low ent.	high ent.	high MI	low MI
human	$91.7_{\pm 1.9}$	$31.7_{\pm 2.9}$	$\Delta 69.3_{\pm 0.9}$	$\Delta 24.7_{\pm 5.0}$
system	$99.0_{\pm 0.0}$	$24.3_{\pm 6.2}$	$\Delta 68.0_{\pm 0.9}$	$\Delta 3.3_{\pm 4.7}$

Table 3: Human and system 'no context' accuracy on lowest and highest entropy questions as well as human and system change in accuracies on lowest and highest mutual information questions.

4 Conclusions

For popular MCMRC datasets, systems can achieve reasonably high performance without performing any comprehension. Without passage information, 'shortcut' systems can confidently determine some correct answer options, eliminate some unlikely distractors, and use general knowledge to gain information. Rather than focusing on average system performance, our work analyses individual question's reliance on world knowledge. We propose a metric based on the shortcut systems to automatically flag questions that are answerable without comprehension. We further provide evidence that the flagged questions are answerable by humans without any context. Lastly, using an approximation of the mutual information, we show that the importance of context varies over the questions in the dataset, and reason that high MI questions can be thought of as candidates for high-quality questions that truly measure comprehension abilities.

5 Limitations

We propose an approach that can automatically flag questions that can be answered without contextual information. However, the remaining questions are not necessarily high-quality questions, since many other aspects make up question quality. Second, the experiments are conducted using only the Electra model, though it is expected similar trends will be picked up by alternative transformer-based language models. Further, exams might be aimed at a level where a lack of specific knowledge may be assumed. Our work does not consider variable candidate knowledge levels, and our evaluation was only done by highly educated (we'd like to think) graduate students. Finally, we acknowledge that our human evaluation was limited in size and questions, however it is clearly demonstrated that for low 'shortcut entropy' questions, comprehension is not necessarily required.

6 Acknowledgements

This research is funded by the EPSRC (The Engineering and Physical Sciences Research Council) Doctoral Training Partnership (DTP) PhD studentship and supported by Cambridge Assessment, University of Cambridge and ALTA.

7 Ethics Statement

There are no serious ethical concerns with this work. The human volunteers all performed the human evaluation tasks willingly without any coercion. The human evaluation took 2 hours per person.

References

J. Charles. Alderson. 2000. *Assessing Reading*, 1 edition. Cambridge University Press,, Cambridge :.

Kevin Clark, Minh-Thang Luong, Quoc V. Le, and Christopher D. Manning. 2020. Electra: Pre-training text encoders as discriminators rather than generators. In *International Conference on Learning Representations*.

Peter Clark, Isaac Cowhey, Oren Etzioni, Tushar Khot, Ashish Sabharwal, Carissa Schoenick, and Oyvind Tafjord. 2018. Think you have solved question answering? try arc, the ai2 reasoning challenge. *ArXiv*, abs/1803.05457.

Antonia Creswell and Murray Shanahan. 2022. Faithful reasoning using large language models. *arXiv preprint arXiv:2208.14271*.

Jacob Devlin, Ming-Wei Chang, Kenton Lee, and Kristina Toutanova. 2019. BERT: Pre-training of deep bidirectional transformers for language understanding. In *Proceedings of the 2019 Conference of the North American Chapter of the Association for Computational Linguistics: Human Language Technologies, Volume 1 (Long and Short Papers)*, pages 4171–4186, Minneapolis, Minnesota. Association for Computational Linguistics.

Chuan Guo, Geoff Pleiss, Yu Sun, and Kilian Q Weinberger. 2017. On calibration of modern neural networks. In *International conference on machine learning*, pages 1321–1330. PMLR.

Lifu Huang, Ronan Le Bras, Chandra Bhagavatula, and Yejin Choi. 2019. Cosmos qa: Machine reading comprehension with contextual commonsense reasoning. In *Proceedings of the 2019 Conference on Empirical Methods in Natural Language Processing and the 9th International Joint Conference on Natural Language Processing (EMNLP-IJCNLP)*, pages 2391–2401.

Robin Jia and Percy Liang. 2017. Adversarial examples for evaluating reading comprehension systems. In *EMNLP*.

Divyansh Kaushik and Zachary C Lipton. 2018. How much reading does reading comprehension require? a critical investigation of popular benchmarks. In *Proceedings of the 2018 Conference on Empirical Methods in Natural Language Processing*, pages 5010–5015.

Guokun Lai, Qizhe Xie, Hanxiao Liu, Yiming Yang, and E. Hovy. 2017. Race: Large-scale reading comprehension dataset from examinations. In *EMNLP*.

Yichan Liang, Jianheng Li, and Jian Yin. 2019. A new multi-choice reading comprehension dataset for curriculum learning. In *Proceedings of The Eleventh Asian Conference on Machine Learning*, volume 101 of *Proceedings of Machine Learning Research*, pages 742–757, Nagoya, Japan. PMLR.

Yinhan Liu, Myle Ott, Naman Goyal, Jingfei Du, Mandar Joshi, Danqi Chen, Omer Levy, M. Lewis, Luke Zettlemoyer, and Veselin Stoyanov. 2019. Roberta: A robustly optimized bert pretraining approach. *International conference on machine learning*, abs/1907.11692.

Richard Yuanzhe Pang, Alicia Parrish, Nitish Joshi, Nikita Nangia, Jason Phang, Angelica Chen, Vishakh Padmakumar, Johnny Ma, Jana Thompson, He He, and Samuel Bowman. 2022. QuALITY: Question answering with long input texts, yes! In *Proceedings of the 2022 Conference of the North American Chapter of the Association for Computational Linguistics: Human Language Technologies*, pages 5336–5358, Seattle, United States. Association for Computational Linguistics.

Vatsal Raina and Mark Gales. 2022. Answer uncertainty and unanswerability in multiple-choice machine reading comprehension. In *Findings of the Association for Computational Linguistics: ACL 2022*, pages 1020–1034, Dublin, Ireland. Association for Computational Linguistics.

Pranav Rajpurkar, Jian Zhang, Konstantin Lopyrev, and Percy Liang. 2016. SQuAD: 100,000+ questions for machine comprehension of text. In *Proceedings of the 2016 Conference on Empirical Methods in Natural Language Processing*, pages 2383–2392, Austin, Texas. Association for Computational Linguistics.

Chenglei Si, Shuohang Wang, Min-Yen Kan, and Jing Jiang. 2019. What does bert learn from multiple-choice reading comprehension datasets? *arXiv preprint arXiv:1910.12391*.

Saku Sugawara, Pontus Stenetorp, Kentaro Inui, and Akiko Aizawa. 2020. Assessing the benchmarking capacity of machine reading comprehension datasets. In *Proceedings of the AAAI Conference on Artificial Intelligence*, volume 34, pages 8918–8927.

Adam Trischler, Tong Wang, Xingdi Yuan, Justin Harris, Alessandro Sordoni, Philip Bachman, and Kaheer Suleman. 2017. Newsqa: A machine comprehension dataset. In *Rep4NLP@ACL*.

Siyuan Wang, Wanjun Zhong, Duyu Tang, Zhongyu Wei, Zhihao Fan, Daxin Jiang, Ming Zhou, and Nan Duan. 2022. Logic-driven context extension and data augmentation for logical reasoning of text. In *Findings of the Association for Computational Linguistics: ACL 2022*, pages 1619–1629.

Ikuya Yamada, Akari Asai, Hiroyuki Shindo, Hideaki Takeda, and Yuji Matsumoto. 2020. Luke: Deep contextualized entity representations with entity-aware self-attention. In *EMNLP*.

Zhilin Yang, Peng Qi, Saizheng Zhang, Yoshua Bengio, William W. Cohen, Ruslan Salakhutdinov, and Christopher D. Manning. 2018. Hotpotqa: A dataset for diverse, explainable multi-hop question answering. In *EMNLP*.

Weihao Yu, Zihang Jiang, Yanfei Dong, and Jiashi Feng. 2020. Reclor: A reading comprehension dataset requiring logical reasoning. In *International Conference on Learning Representations*.

Manzil Zaheer, Guru Guruganesh, Kumar Avinava Dubey, Joshua Ainslie, Chris Alberti, Santiago Ontañón, Philip Pham, Anirudh Ravula, Qifan Wang, Li Yang, and Amr Ahmed. 2020. Big bird: Transformers for longer sequences. *ArXiv*, abs/2007.14062.

Zhuosheng Zhang, Junjie Yang, and Hai Zhao. 2021. Retrospective reader for machine reading comprehension. In *Proceedings of the AAAI Conference on Artificial Intelligence*, volume 35, pages 14506–14514.

Appendix A Additional Results

Appendix A.1 COSMOSQA

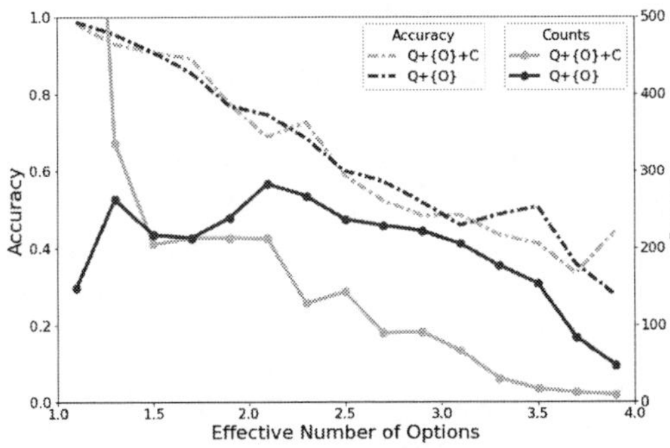

Figure Appendix A.1: Distribution of effective number of options and binned accuracy for COSMOSQA.

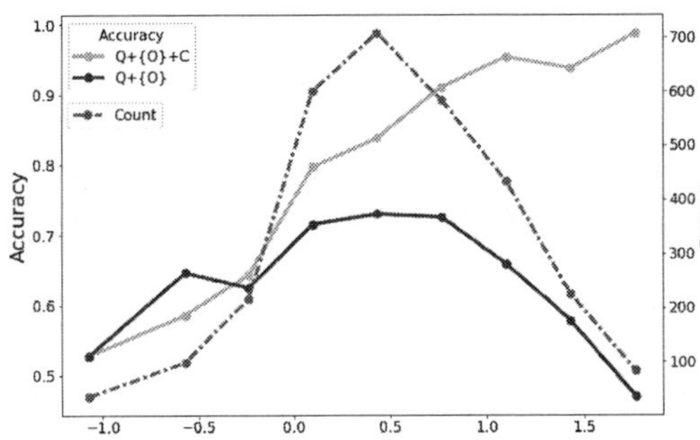

Figure Appendix A.2: Distribution of counts and corresponding accuracy when points are sorted by MI approximation for COSMOSQA.

We repeat the entropy plot (Figure Appendix A.1) for COSMOSQA and find similar trends to those seen in RACE++. The shortcut no-context system has a very flat distribution with a substantial number of questions answerable without context, with the effective number of options again having a clean linear relationship with accuracy. The repeated mutual information plot (Figure Appendix A.2) for COSMOSQA also has the same trend seen in RACE++, validating that our findings are more general that just for RACE++.

Appendix A.2 ReClor

ReClor show roughly the same trends, however the questions of ReClor are much more challenging than in either RACE++ and COSMOSQA, and so we notice that the counts distribution is pushed considerably to the higher entropy side. Additionally, since ReClor is much smaller than RACE++

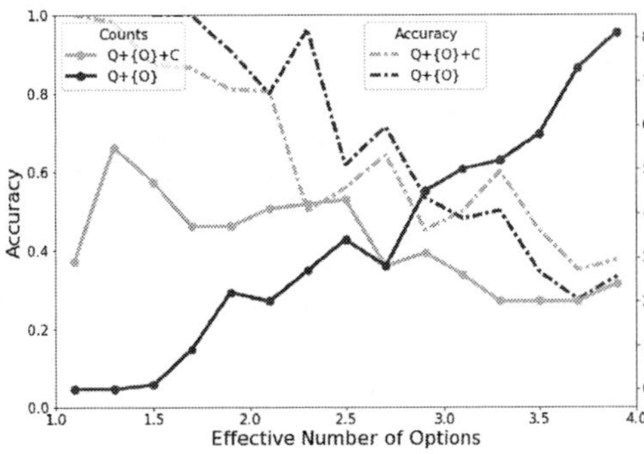

Figure Appendix A.3: Distribution of effective number of options and binned accuracy for ReClor.

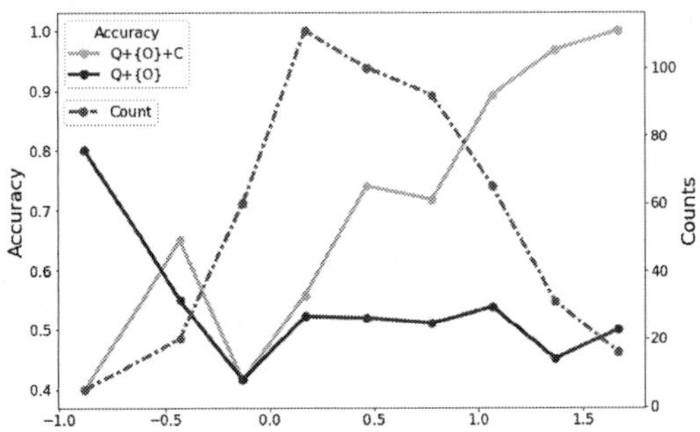

Figure Appendix A.4: Distribution of counts and corresponding accuracy when points are sorted by MI approximation for ReClor.

and COSMOSQA (see Table 1), the curves are less smooth and largely suffer from noise.

Appendix A.3 Other Shortcuts

We also consider other shortcut approaches, such as having context and options (i.e. missing question) and only options (Figure Appendix A.5). Performance of the systems is shown in Table Appendix A.1.

Options only - {O}	[CLS] <Option> [SEP]
Question and Options - Q+{O}	[CLS] <Question> <Option> [SEP]
Option and context - {O}+C	[CLS] <Context> [SEP] <Option> [SEP]
Baseline - Q+{O}+C	[CLS] <Context> [SEP] <Question> <Option> [SEP]

Figure Appendix A.5: System inputs for alternative shortcut systems.

Training data		RACE++	COS.	ReClor
	–	25.00	25.00	25.00
RACE++	{O}	**41.76**	21.44	34.00
	Q+{O}	**57.32**	54.04	34.80
	{O}+C	**68.20**	54.61	46.00
	Q+{O}+C	**85.01**	70.05	48.60
COSMOS	{O}	29.95	**57.39**	25.20
	Q+{O}	38.73	**68.51**	27.80
	{O}+C	52.41	**78.96**	40.40
	Q+{O}+C	66.81	**84.49**	41.20
ReClor	{O}.	26.07	18.29	**49.00**
	Q+{O}	31.27	33.13	**51.80**
	{O}+C	39.83	36.88	**68.40**
	Q+{O}+C	52.69	41.68	**69.80**

Table Appendix A.1: Cross-performance of systems on RACE++, COSMOSQA and ReClor using accuracy.

Appendix B Model Information

B.1 Training Details

For all systems, deep ensembles of 3 models are trained with the large [4] ELECTRA PrLM as a part of the multiple-choice MRC architecture depicted in Figure 2. Each model has 340M parameters. Grid search was performed for hyperparameter tuning with the initial setting of the hyperparameter values dictated by the baseline systems from Yu et al. (2020); Raina and Gales (2022). Apart from the default values used for various hyperparamters, the grid search was performed for the maximum number of epochs $\in \{2, 5, 10\}$; learning rate $\in \{2e-7, 2e-6, 2e-5\}$; batch size $\in \{2, 4\}$. For RACE++, training was performed for 2 epochs at a learning rate of 2e-6 with a batch size of 4 and inputs truncated to 512 tokens. For systems trained on ReClor the final hyperparameter settings included training for 10 epochs at a learning rate of 2e-6 with a batch size of 4 and inputs truncated to 512 tokens. For COSMOSQA, training was performed for 5 epochs at a learning rate of 2e-6 with a batch size of 4 and inputs truncated to 512 tokens. Cross-entropy loss was used at training time with models built using NVIDIA A100 graphical processing units with training time under 3 hours per model for ReClor, 5 hours for COSMOSQA and 4 hours for RACE++. All hyperparameter tuning was performed by training on TRN and selecting values that achieved optimal performance on DEV. For fairness, the 'shortcut' systems (omitting various forms of the input) for each dataset were trained with the same hyperparameter settings as their corresponding baseline systems.

[4]Configuration at: `https://huggingface.co/google/electra-large-discriminator/blob/main/config.json`.

B.2 Evaluation Details

For each dataset, the systems are trained on the training split and hyperparameter tuned on the development split. For RACE++, systems are evaluated on the held out test data, but for COSMOSQA and ReClor, the evaluations are performed on the development split because their test splits have their labels hidden.

B.3 Calibration

The trained models were calibrated post-hoc using single parameter temperature annealing (Guo et al., 2017). Uncalibrated, model probabilities are determined by applying the softmax to the output logit scores s_i:

$$P(y = k; \boldsymbol{\theta}) \propto \exp(s_k) \tag{3}$$

where k denotes a possible output class for a prediction y. Temperature annealing 'softens' the output probability distribution by dividing all logits by a single parameter T before the softmax.

$$P_{CAL}(y = k; \boldsymbol{\theta}) \propto \exp(s_k/T) \tag{4}$$

As the parameter T does not change the relative rankings of the logits, the model's prediction will be unchanged and so temperature scaling does not affect the model's accuracy. The parameter T is chosen such that the accuracy of the system is equal to the mean of the maximum probability (which would be expected for a calibrated system).

Appendix C Licenses

This section details the license agreements of the scientific artifacts used in this work. The dataset COSMOSQA (Huang et al., 2019) has BSD 3-Clause License. The datasets RACE++ (Lai et al., 2017) and ReClor (Yu et al., 2020) are freely available with the limitation on the latter that it can only be used for non-commercial research purposes. Huggingface transformer models are released under: Apache License 2.0. All the scientific aritfacts are consistent with their intended uses.

Appendix D Low Entropy Examples

Make-A-Wish "is a charity to help _ .
A: sick children
B: serious officers
C: famous actors
D: popular singers

What is Google used mainly for?
A: Commanding the gateway.
B: Searching for information.
C: Storing reference books.
D: Providing extra space.

Children with low self-control are more likely to_.
A: become wealthy in later life
B: get good school performance
C: have better financial planning
D: adopt negative behaviors

The word SEASICK means" _ ".
A: to be eager to go to the sea
B: what has nothing to do with the sea
C: to be sick because of the sea
D: that the sea is terrible

The word "scorched" in line 6 is closest in meaning to
A: burned
B: cut
C: enlarged
D: bent

BEVERS: A General, Simple, and Performant Framework for Automatic Fact Verification

Mitchell DeHaven
Information Sciences Institute
University of Southern California
mdehaven@isi.edu

Stephen Scott
University of Nebraska-Lincoln
sscott2@unl.edu

Abstract

Automatic fact verification has become an increasingly popular topic in recent years and among datasets the Fact Extraction and VERification (FEVER) dataset is one of the most popular. In this work we present BEVERS, a tuned baseline system for the FEVER dataset. Our pipeline uses standard approaches for document retrieval, sentence selection, and final claim classification, however, we spend considerable effort ensuring optimal performance for each component. The results are that BEVERS achieves the highest FEVER score and label accuracy among all systems, published or unpublished. We also apply this pipeline to another fact verification dataset, Scifact, and achieve the highest label accuracy among all systems on that dataset as well. We also make our full code available[1].

1 Introduction

The danger of misinformation online has gained significant attention in recent years. This has been reignited by the recent COVID-19 pandemic, where social media sites and other entities were tasked with identifying misleading content or false content to warn users. Being able to develop systems to automate or build tools to improve this process could reduce the need for human annotators to mark content as being misleading or false.

The Fact Extraction and VERification (FEVER) dataset (Thorne et al., 2018) is one the largest and most popular datasets aimed at automated fact verification. The FEVER dataset is comprised of 185,445 claims and uses a 2017 dump of Wikipedia as the corpus to verify the claims, which results in a corpus size of over 5,000,000 articles. For each claim, the task is to find the relevant Wikipedia page(s), the relevant sentence(s) within the page(s), and finally given the relevant sentences and claim determine if the claim is supported, refuted, or there is not enough information. As such, a fairly standard pipeline of a document retrieval system, a sentence selection system, and a final claim classification system is used by most of the systems for the task. The primary metric for the dataset is FEVER score. The FEVER score requires both that the predicted label is correct as well as at least one piece of correct evidence being retrieved as predicted evidence.

Much of the recent work has examined parts of the pipeline and made novel improvements over baseline approaches. For our system, rather than making novel improvements against the baseline pipeline, we instead tune each of these components to ensure maximum performance. In fact, our pipeline is quite similar to one of the first FEVER systems to utilize Transformer models (Soleimani et al., 2020). We call our system Baseline fact Extraction and VERification System (BEVERS). Despite its relative simplicity, our system attains state of the art (SOTA) performance on the FEVER blind test set. When applying our baseline pipeline to another popular fact verification dataset, Scifact (Wadden et al., 2020), our system achieves the highest label F1 score on that dataset as well.

2 Related Work and Methods

2.1 Document Retrieval

The initial baseline for FEVER (Thorne et al., 2018) utilized a standard TF-IDF document retrieval model. Hanselowski et al. (2018) improved on this by using named entity recognition (NER) to extract query terms from the claim text and query those terms against WikiMedia's API[2], which has become widely used among other systems. Recently systems such as those from Stammbach (2021) and Jiang et al. (2021) have used a combination of traditional IR approaches with Hanselowski et al.'s (2018) NER approach. We follow a sim-

[1] https://github.com/mitchelldehaven/bevers

[2] https://www.mediawiki.org/wiki/API:Main_page

Proceedings of the Sixth Fact Extraction and VERification Workshop (FEVER), pages 58–65
May 5, 2023

ilar setup, however, we replace the approach of Hanselowski et al.'s (2018) use of WikiMedia's API. We similarly extract named entities to form query terms, however, we run those against a fuzzy string search system using the titles of the documents. For our TF-IDF, we build separate representations for documents and titles. This is for two reasons. First, it allows us to separately optimize the parameters for titles and documents. Second, it forces the retrieval system to give titles more attention as it is forced to retrieve half of all documents based on the title alone. We give an ablation over these design decisions in Appendix B.

2.2 Sentence Selection

After retrieving documents, the next step is to score evidence and form a ranking for the predicted evidence of the claim. The simplest approach to doing this is referred to as "point-wise" ranking, in which each sentence is scored individually against the claim. This is the approach utilized by most systems. Soleimani et al. (2020) looked at improving on this utilizing a pairwise approach to ranking. Stammbach (2021) found that utilizing document-wide context via sparse attention Transformers improves on point-wise approaches. Our system utilizes a simple point-wise approach to sentence selection to form the predicted evidence. We look at two cases, treating the task as both a binary classification task and a ternary classification task. In the binary case, the label set is simply RELEVANT and IRRELEVANT with the softmax score of RELEVANT being used for ranking. In the ternary case, we use REFUTES, NOT ENOUGH INFO, and SUPPORTS as the labels and use 1− NOT ENOUGH INFO softmax score for ranking. We randomly sample sentences from the document retrieved from our document retrieval approach for negative samples. In the binary case, these random negative samples are assigned to the IRRELEVANT label class and all true evidence is assigned to RELEVANT. In the ternary case, the negative samples are assigned to NOT ENOUGH INFO, and the true evidence is assigned to its respective labels, REFUTES and SUPPORTS.

In addition, we utilize a process we call evidence-based re-retrieval. The FEVER dataset includes hyperlink information for each sentence in the dataset. This process takes the initial set of predicted evidence for a claim and extracts additional documents based on hyperlinks found in the initial sentences retrieved. Sentences from these additional documents are scored and combined with the initial sentences to form a final top 5 predicted evidence. This process is very similar to Stammbach's (2021) "multi-hop retrieval", with slight differences in how sentences are discounted when combining the two sets of sentences. Stammbach sets evidence from re-retrieved documents just above a predefined threshold for selection to prevent re-retrieved evidence from pushing evidence from the initial retrieval outside of the top 5. We similarly found that simply combining both sets together actually hurts recall, because evidence from re-retrieval sometimes pushes out relevant evidence from the initial retrieval. In our approach, we scale the sentence selection scores of the re-retrieved sentences by the score of the original sentence that was responsible for its retrieval. Thus, if evidence s_j was retrieved due to a hyperlink in s_i the final retrieval score is $score(s_i) \times score(s_j)$. Scaling this way reduces re-retrieved evidence pushing evidence from the initial retrieval from the top-5 selection. It also allows re-retrieved evidence scores to be proportional to the score of the initial evidence responsible for its retrieval.

2.3 Claim Classification

The claim classification portion has recently seen the most diversity in approaches to the task. The initial Transformer approach of Soleimani et al. (2020) formed predictions for each claim and evidence pair, using a simple set of rules to aggregate labels across the different pieces of evidence. Subsequently, several works examined the use of graph neural networks as the claim classification model (Liu et al., 2020; Zhong et al., 2020), showing improvements over simply using Transformers due to their ability to aggregate information over different pieces of evidence. More recently, increasing the size of the Transformer models and concatenating all evidence sentences together have shown further improvements, with Jiang et al. (2021) using T5 (Raffel et al., 2020) and Stammbach (2021) using DeBERTa V2 XL MNLI (He et al., 2021). Finally, the previous SOTA among public systems, ProofVER (Krishna et al., 2022), utilizes natural language proofs generated via seq2seq models for interpretable inference steps.

For our approach, we look at prediction over singleton, concatenated, and a mixed case. We predict a top-5 evidence set for each claim for training us-

Hyperparameter	Values
Force Lowercase	True, False
Force ASCII	True, False
Norm	L2, None
Sublinear TF	True, False
Max Ngram	1, 2

Table 1: The hyperparameter search for our TF-IDF system.

Hyperparameter	Values
Label Set	binary, ternary
Negative Samples	5, 10, 20, 40
Learning Rate	1e-5, 6e-6, 3e-6
Label Smoothing	0.0, 0.1, 0.2

Table 2: The hyperparameter search our sentence selection model.

ing our document selection and sentence selection. In the singleton case, we generate a prediction for each piece of evidence using as input the $\langle$claim, evidence$\rangle$ pairs. In the concatenated case, we concatenate all the evidence together and form the input based on $\langle$claim, evidence$_1$, evidence$_2, \ldots\rangle$. For the mixed approach, we mix the singleton approach and concatenated approach together. For the singleton and mixed approach, we have multiple predictions for each claim. To aggregate these into a single score, we use the softmax scores for each prediction with the retrieval scores and train a gradient boosting classifier (Friedman, 2001) on these inputs to produce a single prediction. In the singleton case, the input is a 5×4 matrix (5 pieces of evidence, 3 softmax scores and a retrieval score). In the mixed case, the input is a 6×4 matrix (includes the additional concatenated input softmax scores and the retrieval score, computed from the average retrieval scores of the 5 pieces of evidence). The singleton and concatenated approaches have been used previously (Soleimani et al., 2020; Jiang et al., 2021), while we are not aware of any works that look at simply mixing these approaches together.

3 Experimental Setup

What we believe to be the source of improvements for our system is hyperparameter tuning for each component. We identify hyperparameters and potential values and run a grid search to find the optimal configurations for each component. In this section, we will go over each of the grid searches

Hyperparameter	Values
Learning Rate	0.1, 0.3
Estimators	20, 40, 60, 80, 100
Max Depth	2, 4, 6, 8

Table 3: The hyperparameter search our gradient boosting model.

providing additional details on the exact setup.

For our TF-IDF system, we utilize SciKit Learn's (Pedregosa et al., 2011) TF-IDF representation. In Table 1 we list the hyperparameters and their candidate values used in the grid search. We use recall @ 5 on the development set for finding the best configuration. The fuzzy string search is implemented using Sqlite's spellfix1 virtual table[3]. We set a simple edit distance threshold for retrieving additional documents.

Our sentence selection hyperparameter tuning is split into two sections. First, we optimize the number of negative samples selected as well as binary vs ternary classes for ranking. Since the FEVER dataset does not provide evidence for NOT ENOUGH INFO claims, negative samples must be used to generate training examples for these. Using the best selection from the initial setup, we tune the learning rate and label smoothing. The candidate values for the tuning can be found in Table 2. Given the imbalance in the training set and the balanced nature of the dev and test set, we oversample the minority classes so that label distribution in the training set matches that of the dev and test sets. We use the dev set for determining optimal hyperparameter values. RoBERTa Large (Liu et al., 2019) is used as the initial model for fine-tuning.

The claim classification tuning setup is quite similar to sentence selection. We initially tune the learning rate and label smoothing using the same candidate values for the concatenated case. Instead of tuning the model types of singleton, concatenated, and mixed, we simply use the best hyperparameter configuration and train a model for each of these to draw final comparisons. Again, given the imbalance in classes in the train set, we use class weighting to compensate for this imbalance. For fine-tuning we use RoBERTa Large MNLI and DeBERTa V2 XL MNLI.

Finally, for the singleton and mixed approaches, we use XGBoost (Chen and Guestrin, 2016) for training a classifier to aggregate the predictions

[3]https://www.sqlite.org/spellfix1.html

System	Test LA	Test FEVER
Soleimani et al. (2020)	71.86%	69.66%
KGAT Liu et al. (2020)	74.07%	70.38%
LisT5 Jiang et al. (2021)	79.35%	75.87%
Stammbach (2021)	79.20%	76.80%
ProoFVer Krishna et al. (2022)	79.47 %	76.82%
Ours (RoBERTa Large MNLI) singleton	78.01%	76.09%
Ours (RoBERTa Large MNLI) concatenated	79.14%	76.69%
Ours (RoBERTa Large MNLI) mixed	79.39%	76.89%
Ours (DeBERTa V2 XL MNLI) mixed	**80.24%**	**77.70%**

Table 4: Full system comparison for label accuracy (LA) and FEVER score on the blind test set.

into a single prediction. Similarly, we define a hyperparameter grid to find the optimal values. Since the previous steps were all trained on the train set and thus the softmax scores and retrieval scores will be overly optimistic on the training set, we instead train the XGBoost classifier on the dev set. We use 4-fold cross-validation to find the optimal configuration.

4 Results

System	Dev Recall @ 5
Hanselowski et al. (2018)	87.10%
Liu et al. (2020)	94.37%
Soleimani et al. (2020)	88.38%
Jiang et al. (2021)	90.54%
Stammbach (2021)	93.62%
Ours	92.03%
+ re-retrieval	**94.41%**

Table 5: The results of several sentence selection systems in terms of recall @ 5 on the dev set.

For sentence selection, the primary metric used is recall @ 5. This is due to the fact that when computing FEVER score, the scoring metric will only consider up to 5 pieces of predicted evidence. In Table 5 we compare our sentence selection system against several other top systems on the dev set. As can be seen, our sentence selection system outperforms all previous systems in terms of recall @ 5 on the dev set. This is despite using a substantially smaller model relative to Jiang et al.'s (2021) T5 approach as well as only using pointwise scoring for sentence selection as opposed to Stammbach's (2021) full document context approach. We separate our results from using initial retrieval and including evidence-based re-retrieval, which shows a very large improvement in recall by doing re-retrieval, consistent with Stammbach's (2021) findings.

For claim classification results, we present the entire end-to-end results for our system in Table 4. The simple approach of mixing the singleton and concatenate approaches gives a small improvement, although is not a substantial source of improvement. Despite the singleton approach being incapable of modeling claims that require multi-hop evidence, it still performs well. Despite using a relatively smaller model of 300 million parameters when compared to 3 billion with T5 and 900 million with DeBERTa V2 XL MNLI, our RoBERT Large MNLI system achieves the highest FEVER score among all published systems. When we utilize DeBERTa V2 XL MNLI using our mixed approach, we achieve the highest label accuracy and FEVER score amongst all systems, published or unpublished, on the blind test set.

5 Beyond FEVER: Scifact

System	SS + L	Abstract LO
Pradeep et al. (2021)	58.8	64.9
Zhang et al. (2021)	63.1	68.1
Wadden et al. (2022)	**67.2**	72.5
Ours	58.1	**73.2**

Table 6: System comparison for SS + L F1 score and Abstract LO F1 score on SciFact blind test set.

To test this pipeline for automatic fact verification beyond the FEVER dataset, we also apply these methods to the SciFact dataset (Wadden et al., 2020). SciFact is very similar in structure to the FEVER dataset, however, the corpus is composed of scientific articles. A source of difficulty is that claims are often phrased in lay terms, which can be a stark difference in form from how topics are presented in scientific articles. The overall size of the dataset is quite a bit smaller as well, containing only 1,409 claims and 5,183 article abstracts, which serve as the corpus. Despite this, we keep our pipeline nearly identical to FEVER, excluding only the fuzzy string search component. We follow the approach of Wadden et al. (2022) for improving the initial models for finetuning given the low resource nature of the dataset.

We show the results of our pipeline in Table 6 compared to the current SOTA (Wadden et al., 2022) and other top systems. The metrics reported are sentence selection + label (SS + L) and abstract label only (Abstract LO). These metrics roughly correspond to FEVER Score and label accuracy for FEVER. As can be seen in the SS + L metric, the simplicity of our document retrieval system appears to hold the overall system back. Our system only uses TF-IDF whereas the three others add neural rerankers on top of their retrieval. Despite this, on the Abstract LO metric our system achieves the highest F1 score on the blind test set, outperforming the SOTA on this metric.

6 Conclusion

We presented BEVERS, a strong baseline approach for the FEVER and SciFact datasets. Despite being similar to previous works in structure (Soleimani et al., 2020) and utilizing little in terms of novel improvements, our system was able to achieve SOTA performance on FEVER and the highest label accuracy on SciFact. We primarily attribute these improvements to diligent hyperparameter tuning and error analysis. While several previous works have shown novel contributions to portions of the pipeline can yield improvements, in this work we show a well-tuned baseline is very strong.

7 Limitations

As shown with SciFact, this pipeline struggles in situations where there is a mismatch in how claims are phrased and how evidence is phrased in the corpus. Since our retrieval method is term-based, synonymous terms are often missed, and thus in such systems utilizing neural retrieval methods will offer better performance. In addition, this work does not thoroughly examine which design decisions or approaches led to the improvements seen in this pipeline. We note that evidence-based re-retrieval does give substantial improvements, yet even without re-retrieval, our sentence selection outperforms most previous systems by a substantial margin, so it is not the sole source of improvement.

References

Tianqi Chen and Carlos Guestrin. 2016. XGBoost: A scalable tree boosting system. In *Proceedings of the 22nd ACM SIGKDD International Conference on Knowledge Discovery and Data Mining*, KDD '16, pages 785–794, New York, NY, USA. ACM.

Jerome H. Friedman. 2001. Greedy function approximation: A gradient boosting machine. *The Annals of Statistics*, 29(5):1189 – 1232.

Andreas Hanselowski, Hao Zhang, Zile Li, Daniil Sorokin, Benjamin Schiller, Claudia Schulz, and Iryna Gurevych. 2018. UKP-athene: Multi-sentence textual entailment for claim verification. In *Proceedings of the First Workshop on Fact Extraction and VERification (FEVER)*, pages 103–108, Brussels, Belgium. Association for Computational Linguistics.

Pengcheng He, Xiaodong Liu, Jianfeng Gao, and Weizhu Chen. 2021. Deberta: Decoding-enhanced bert with disentangled attention. In *International Conference on Learning Representations*.

Kelvin Jiang, Ronak Pradeep, and Jimmy Lin. 2021. Exploring listwise evidence reasoning with t5 for fact verification. In *Proceedings of the 59th Annual Meeting of the Association for Computational Linguistics and the 11th International Joint Conference on Natural Language Processing (Volume 2: Short Papers)*, pages 402–410, Online. Association for Computational Linguistics.

Amrith Krishna, Sebastian Riedel, and Andreas Vlachos. 2022. ProoFVer: Natural logic theorem proving for fact verification. *Transactions of the Association for Computational Linguistics*, 10:1013–1030.

Yinhan Liu, Myle Ott, Naman Goyal, Jingfei Du, Mandar Joshi, Danqi Chen, Omer Levy, Mike Lewis, Luke Zettlemoyer, and Veselin Stoyanov. 2019. Roberta: A robustly optimized bert pretraining approach.

Zhenghao Liu, Chenyan Xiong, Maosong Sun, and Zhiyuan Liu. 2020. Fine-grained fact verification with kernel graph attention network. In *Proceedings of the 58th Annual Meeting of the Association for Computational Linguistics*, pages 7342–7351, Online. Association for Computational Linguistics.

F. Pedregosa, G. Varoquaux, A. Gramfort, V. Michel, B. Thirion, O. Grisel, M. Blondel, P. Prettenhofer, R. Weiss, V. Dubourg, J. Vanderplas, A. Passos, D. Cournapeau, M. Brucher, M. Perrot, and E. Duchesnay. 2011. Scikit-learn: Machine learning in Python. *Journal of Machine Learning Research*, 12:2825–2830.

Ronak Pradeep, Xueguang Ma, Rodrigo Nogueira, and Jimmy Lin. 2021. Scientific claim verification with VerT5erini. In *Proceedings of the 12th International Workshop on Health Text Mining and Information Analysis*, pages 94–103, online. Association for Computational Linguistics.

Colin Raffel, Noam Shazeer, Adam Roberts, Katherine Lee, Sharan Narang, Michael Matena, Yanqi Zhou, Wei Li, and Peter J. Liu. 2020. Exploring the limits of transfer learning with a unified text-to-text transformer. *J. Mach. Learn. Res.*, 21(1).

Amir Soleimani, Christof Monz, and Marcel Worring. 2020. Bert for evidence retrieval and claim verification. In *Advances in Information Retrieval: 42nd European Conference on IR Research, ECIR 2020, Lisbon, Portugal, April 14–17, 2020, Proceedings, Part II*, page 359–366, Berlin, Heidelberg. Springer-Verlag.

Dominik Stammbach. 2021. Evidence selection as a token-level prediction task. In *Proceedings of the Fourth Workshop on Fact Extraction and VERification (FEVER)*, pages 14–20, Dominican Republic. Association for Computational Linguistics.

James Thorne, Andreas Vlachos, Christos Christodoulopoulos, and Arpit Mittal. 2018. FEVER: a large-scale dataset for fact extraction and VERification. In *Proceedings of the 2018 Conference of the North American Chapter of the Association for Computational Linguistics: Human Language Technologies, Volume 1 (Long Papers)*, pages 809–819, New Orleans, Louisiana. Association for Computational Linguistics.

David Wadden, Shanchuan Lin, Kyle Lo, Lucy Lu Wang, Madeleine van Zuylen, Arman Cohan, and Hannaneh Hajishirzi. 2020. Fact or fiction: Verifying scientific claims. In *Proceedings of the 2020 Conference on Empirical Methods in Natural Language Processing (EMNLP)*, pages 7534–7550, Online. Association for Computational Linguistics.

David Wadden, Kyle Lo, Lucy Wang, Arman Cohan, Iz Beltagy, and Hannaneh Hajishirzi. 2022. MultiVerS: Improving scientific claim verification with weak supervision and full-document context. In *Findings of the Association for Computational Linguistics: NAACL 2022*, pages 61–76, Seattle, United States. Association for Computational Linguistics.

Deming Ye, Yankai Lin, Jiaju Du, Zhenghao Liu, Peng Li, Maosong Sun, and Zhiyuan Liu. 2020. Coreferential Reasoning Learning for Language Representation. In *Proceedings of the 2020 Conference on Empirical Methods in Natural Language Processing (EMNLP)*, pages 7170–7186, Online. Association for Computational Linguistics.

Zhiwei Zhang, Jiyi Li, Fumiyo Fukumoto, and Yanming Ye. 2021. Abstract, rationale, stance: A joint model for scientific claim verification. In *Proceedings of the 2021 Conference on Empirical Methods in Natural Language Processing*, pages 3580–3586, Online and Punta Cana, Dominican Republic. Association for Computational Linguistics.

Wanjun Zhong, Jingjing Xu, Duyu Tang, Zenan Xu, Nan Duan, Ming Zhou, Jiahai Wang, and Jian Yin. 2020. Reasoning over semantic-level graph for fact checking. In *Proceedings of the 58th Annual Meeting of the Association for Computational Linguistics*, pages 6170–6180, Online. Association for Computational Linguistics.

A Optimal Hyperparameter Settings

In Table 7 we show the optimal hyperparameter settings for the various TF-IDF configurations. To minimize space, we use "Cat" to refer to the concatenated TF-IDF setup. In Table 8 and Table 9 we show the optimal hyperparameter values for sentence selection and claim classification models. Finally, in Table 10 we include the optimal hyperparameter values for the XGBoost classifier.

Hyperparameter	Cat	Title, Document
Force Lowercase	True	True, False
Force ASCII	True	True, True
Norm	None	L2, None
Sublinear TF	True	True, True
Max Ngram	2	2, 2

Table 7: Optimal hyperparameters for the concatenated and separated TF-IDF configurations.

Hyperparameter	Optimal Value
Label Set	Ternary
Negative Samples	10
Learning Rate	3e-6
Label Smoothing	0.0

Table 8: Optimal hyperparameters for sentence selection model.

Hyperparameter	Optimal Value
Learning Rate	3e-6
Label Smoothing	0.2

Table 9: Optimal hyperparameters for claim classification model.

B Ablation Studies

In Table 11 we show the impacts of various design choices for document retrieval and their impacts on sentence selection. We use our best sentence

Hyperparameter	Optimal Value
Max Depth	2
Number of Estimators	60
Learning Rate	0.3

Table 10: Optimal hyperparameters for XGBoost aggregation classifier.

selection model for ranking the sentences retrieved by the document retrieval approaches. Previous works use OFEVER from the original paper as a metric for comparing document retrieval methods, however, OFEVER does not account for different approaches retrieving different numbers of documents given that is an oracle approach. Thus, we find measuring the sentence selection in this way gives a better representation of improvements.

Retrieval Approach	Dev Recall @ 5
TF-IDF (concatenated)	84.49 %
+ fuzzy string search	91.35 %
+ document re-retrieval	93.58 %
TF-IDF (separated)	87.09 %
+ fuzzy string search	92.03 %
+ document re-retrieval	**94.41**%

Table 11: Dev set recall @ 5 using various document retrieval approaches.

In Table 12 we compare our claim classification setup with KGAT's. Rather than utilizing our document retrieval and sentence selection, we use KGAT's sentence selection outputs which they make publicly available. This allows for a more direct comparison since we are using the same evidence for forming predictions. The only changes we make: re-score the top 5 evidence from KGAT's sentence selection using our own best sentence selection model and re-train the gradient boosting classifier. Despite using the same evidence as KGAT, our claim classification still outperforms using either RoBERTa Large or RoBERTa Large MNLI. So while some of the improvement in our system is attributable to improvements in document retrieval and sentence selection our approach to claim classification still outperforms previous systems when using the same retrieval outputs.

Author (Model)	Test LA	Test FEVER
KGAT (RoBERTa Large) (Liu et al., 2020)	74.07 %	70.38 %
KGAT (CorefRoBERTa) (Ye et al., 2020)	75.96 %	72.30 %
Ours (RoBERTa Large)	76.60 %	73.21 %
Ours (RoBERTa Large MNLI)	77.95 %	74.08 %

Table 12: Comparison between KGAT's claim classification and ours. We use KGAT's released outputs for evidence retrieval, so differences in performance are not attributable to improvements in our system's retrieval approach.

An Effective Approach for Informational and Lexical Bias Detection

Iffat Maab[1], Edison Marrese-Taylor[1,2], Yutaka Matsuo[1]
[1]The University of Tokyo
[2]National Institute of Advanced Industrial Science and Technology
{iffatmaab, emarrese, matsuo}@weblab.t.u-tokyo.ac.jp

Abstract

In this paper we present a thorough investigation of automatic bias recognition on BASIL, a dataset of political news which has been annotated with different kinds of biases. We begin by unveiling several inconsistencies in prior work using this dataset, showing that most approaches focus only on certain task formulations while ignoring others, and also failing to report important evaluation details. We provide a comprehensive categorization of these approaches, as well as a more uniform and clear set of evaluation metrics. We argue about the importance of the missing formulations and also propose the novel task of simultaneously detecting different kinds of biases in news. In our work, we tackle bias on six different BASIL classification tasks in a unified manner. Eventually, we introduce a simple yet effective approach based on data augmentation and preprocessing which is generic and works very well across models and task formulations, allowing us to obtain state-of-the-art results. We also perform ablation studies on some tasks to quantify the strength of data augmentation and preprocessing, and find that they correlate positively on all bias tasks.

1 Introduction

News outlets have expanded to become one of the most influential and prominent platforms within mass media. News articles play a central role in transforming individual and public opinion (Hamborg et al., 2019). Public opinion of journalists influence viewers to become biased towards a particular issue. The consequence of media bias is massive, and raises questions about the credibility of news. For example, Bernhardt et al. (2008) reported that media bias led to the election of the wrong candidate, and according to Wolton (2019), voters are always well-informed with unbiased rather than biased media outlets. Moreover, biased media outlets have also been found to provide less information, which reduces voter's welfare Duggan and Martinelli (2011).

Misinformation has enormous potential in changing the individual and public beliefs, expectations, or desired conclusions. The harmful biases contained in news media require rigorous analysis to be detected and quantified, but once addressing these issues can improve the quality of research process to maximize the accuracy and credibility of research results (Johnson et al., 2020). To enhance transparency and reliability in promoting accurate information, it is important to realize bias in machine learning methods and how humans perceive bias (Sun et al., 2019).

Seminal work by Fan et al. (2019) has been a key contribution in bias detection in news, with the introduction of the BASIL dataset. Critically, to the best of our knowledge, this dataset is the first to be annotated with different kinds of bias. This is due to the fact that, as pointed out by Fan et al. (2019), some kinds of bias can only be analyzed in a broader context, because a given sentence becomes ambiguous in isolation at any given time. In this sense, their proposal was to differentiate *informational bias* from *lexical bias*. On one hand, the former is usually presented using speculative, imperative, and tangential clauses that convey information in a factual and neutral way (van den Berg and Markert, 2020) to sway readers' opinions towards news entities (Guo and Zhu, 2022a), therefore depending mostly on the context. On the other hand, lexical bias instead depends on linguistic attributes like word choice and syntax and originates from content realization or how things or events are expressed, and is generally not depending on the context (Greene and Resnik, 2009; Hube and Fetahu, 2019; Iyyer et al., 2014; Yano et al., 2010; Recasens et al., 2013). Table 1 shows examples of informational and lexical bias on New York Times (NYT) news (2nyt; source: nyt, event: 2) on the BASIL dataset. The three sentences report

Proceedings of the Sixth Fact Extraction and VERification Workshop (FEVER), pages 66–77
May 5, 2023 ©2023 Association for Computational Linguistics

Bias	Polarity	Sentence	Index #
Informational	Neg	**The president again suggested that he should win the Nobel Peace Prize, and he reviewed which conservative commentators had been supportive of him, while dismissing Ann Coulter, who has not.**	10
Lexical	Neg	Sounding alternately **defensive and aggrieved**, Mr. Trump explained his failure to secure wall funding during his first two years in office when Republicans controlled both houses of Congress by saying, I was a little new to the job.	11
Neutral	*None*	He blamed certain people, a particular one, for not having pushed this faster, a clear reference to former Speaker Paul D. Ryan of Wisconsin, a Republican.	12

Table 1: Examples extracted from BASIL dataset, from New York Times (NYT) section and discussing the same event, showing how informational and lexical bias manifest. In the examples, text spans annotated with informational bias and lexical bias are highlighted in bold, and we refer to sentences annotated with no bias as 'Neutral'.

on Donald Trump as the main event. As seen, informational bias covers the article context broadly, often depending on the complete sentence, whereas lexical bias is expressed in polarized words as highlighted.

Though the development of datasets such as BASIL has brought an interesting new paradigm to look at bias in news, thereby drawing the attention of several members of the research community and leading to abundant prior work, we note that these studies mostly focus on informational bias only (van den Berg and Markert, 2020; Guo and Zhu, 2022b; Fan et al., 2019; Lei et al., 2022), with lexical bias studied solely by Fan et al. (2019). While we surmise that this could be partially due to the fact that lexical bias appears comparatively less frequently in news articles, making the automatic detection of both kinds of bias simultaneously difficult, we think this should be no reason to focus on either and argue that detecting lexical bias from informational bias should be equally significant. In this context, our take is well-aligned with previous work by Zhou and Bansal (2020), who highlighted the uniqueness of lexical bias and demonstrated its importance through several experiments.

In light of this issue, in our work, we propose approaches to detect both informational and lexical bias simultaneously. Our holistic view on bias detection enables us to reveal important trade-offs between informational and lexical bias, and we perform a sensitivity analysis of such trade-offs in various task formulations. Based on our findings, we propose a set of data augmentation techniques which we combine with deep learning models to improve performance.

Furthermore, our focus on both bias detection problems leads us to propose more clear and consistent task formulations. Specifically, we note out several inconsistencies in the reporting of performance on previous work, and provide a framework to improve uniformity and clarity, and to avoid problems we found in prior work. Consequently, we highlighted incoherent task formulations of bias classification tasks, absence of a significant task of detecting both informational and lexical bias simultaneously, and missing evaluation metrics of bias interpreted labels. Our findings are connected to a related issue which has been brought to attention by van den Berg and Markert (2020), showing that sentence-based splits can introduce data leakage since labeled sentences from the same or similar articles can appear in training and test subsets, resulting in overestimation of the predicting accuracy. Our proposed framework not only enables us to adequately compare our results with previous work, which we often find lacks structure in this sense, but also helps pave the way for future research involving the BASIL dataset. In summary, our work provides the following contributions:

1. We unveil and remove inconsistencies in prior work, providing uniform and more clear evaluation metrics with various task formulations on BASIL.

2. To the best of our knowledge, we are the first to propose the task of simultaneously detecting both informational and lexical bias, and

distinguish them from neutral examples. We propose models to tackle this new task and establish its importance in overall bias detection problem setting.

3. We propose an approach based on data augmentation and preprocessing which is generic and works well across a selection of models and settings in bias detection in news, allowing us to obtain state-of-the-art results on BASIL.

2 Related work

There has been a growing interest in the investigation of linguistic information presented by neural models (Liu et al., 2019a). A study by Jia et al. (2019) worked on the bias and distortion of online commentary information based on online reviews, and illustrate online review components significance over increased reputation and false reviews. Hovy and Prabhumoye (2021) study five sources of bias including data, annotation process, input representations, models, and research design where research design is the most difficult to detect because it requires systematic analysis and subjectivity of human perceptions.

The work on BASIL dataset in the literature is not exhaustive to the best of our knowledge. BASIL dataset provided by Fan et al. (2019) use BERT and RoBERTa for informational and lexical bias detection while treating sentences in isolation, whereas informational bias is also explored with different types of contexts like textual, article, event and domain using BiLSTM's, BERT and Event Context-Inclusive Model (EvCIM) inspired by Context Aware Model of Papalampidi et al. (2019), we will omit a detailed explanation of these models, referring readers to (van den Berg and Markert, 2020). Fan et al. (2019) demonstrate that informational bias is more challenging to detect due to its dependence on content selection as compared to lexical bias. Another study by Lee et al. (2021) introduce a general purpose misinformation UnifiedM2 model for bias detection in BASIL and handle tasks like fake news, clickbait and rumors. Contrastive learning and Graph Attention Network in the MultiCTX (Multi-level ConTeXt) model uses triplets of BASIL to detect informational bias as proposed by Guo and Zhu (2022b). Similarly, bias sentence identification is also studied by Lei et al. (2022) through local and global discourse structures using RoBERTa for addressing bias. We compare our results with the aforementioned current state-of-the-art methods to investigate the significance of our proposed approach.

Another topic relevant to our work is data augmentation. In general, data augmentation in NLP is at an emerging stage compared to Computer Vision (Shorten et al., 2021; Shleifer, 2019). Among data augmentation techniques in NLP one that has recently shown excellent results in the context of machine translation is backtranslation (Sennrich et al., 2015). The idea is to pair monolingual data with an automatic backtranslation generated by a given model or external system, which led to considerable performance improvements on neural machine translation, showing that even for small amounts of in domain monolingual data, backtranslation is effective for domain adaptation. More recently, Edunov et al. (2018) scale backtranslation to hundreds of millions of monolingual sentences and achieve substantial improvements. The same approach is more recently been successfully adapted to other task. For example, Shleifer (2019) focus on sentiment classification and use backtranslation on only 500 examples, obtaining an 8.1% improvement over the augmentation-free baseline based on ULMFit (Howard and Ruder, 2018) on the IMDB dataset. Our work is similar to this, but we adapt the approach for bias detection.

Finally, our work is related to stemming, the process of linguistic normalization where variant forms of a word are converted to a stem or root word. There are different methods for stemming, but most of them follow a rule-based or linguistic approach, each one with its own advantages and limitations (Jivani et al., 2011). Relevant for us is the fact that stemming has been shown to add semantic value in feature selection, as for example Biba and Gjati (2014) proved that stemming of composite words greatly improves classification of fake news. Moreover, Mahendra et al. (2021) showed that cleaning and stemming resulted in the greatest model performance on the medical domain for the task in mortality prediction on ICU (Intensive Care Unit) patients. We refer readers to a thorough survey of stemmers spanning over the past 50 years by Singh and Gupta (2016).

3 Proposed Approach

The Bias Annotation Spans on the Informational Level (BASIL) dataset, provided by Fan et al. (2019), is based on three news sources, i.e., Huffington Post (HPO), Fox News (FOX), and New York Times (NYT) from 2010 to 2019, containing 300 news articles with 100 triplets of news articles taken from each news source. BASIL contains both binary sentence classification labels of informational and lexical bias together with span level annotations for token classification. An isolated sentence is biased if it contains at least one bias span. There are 7,977 sentences in BASIL having 1,249 sentences with informational and 478 sentences with lexical bias (Fan et al., 2019). BASIL has more prevalence of informational bias than lexical bias. It covers news articles of reasonable time i.e., 10 years, representing conservative from FOX, neutral from NYT, and liberal from HPO, respectively.

Since informational bias is presented in a factual and neutral way, there is increasing prevalence of informational bias in news media, as evidenced by Fan et al. (2019). This factual reporting of informational bias makes its prediction more challenging on a sentence level. On the other hand, lexical bias is reportedly easier to capture because of its non-contextual nature, depending mostly on word choice (Chen et al., 2020). For example, a study on Tagalog-speaking Filipino pre-school children by Devanadera and Alieto (2019) showed that lexical bias is related to lexical inventories like nouns, verbs and adjectives produced by young children, with nouns as the leading or dominant lexical bias among children in their narrative production. Despite these facts, the detection of both types of bias remains a difficult and challenging task, as evidenced by the study on BASIL performed by Chen et al. (2020), which includes approaches for the automatic detection of both types of bias (although not distinguishing them).

BASIL has 7,977 sentences, from which 1,249 and 478 are labeled as containing with informational bias and lexical bias, respectively. Following the formulation of Fan et al. (2019), this leads to 6,250 sentences with no bias. After careful consideration of models proposed in prior work utilizing BASIL, we note inconsistencies in the task formulation across papers, which are derived from the way in which these labels are interpreted and used.

In order to shed light into this issue, we begin by organizing prior work and defining the notation we will utilize in the rest of the manuscript, for the sake of simplicity. We refer to sentences annotated with no bias as **'NEU'**, sentences annotated with

LABELS	Baseline					
	Fan	**Berg**	**Lee**	**Guo**	**Lei**	**Ours**
INF v/s LEX	-	-	-	-	-	✓
INF v/s NEU	✓	-	-	-	-	✓
INF v/s OTH	-	✓	-	✓	✓	✓
LEX v/s NEU	✓	-	-	-	-	✓
BIAS v/s NEU	-	-	✓	-	-	✓
INF v/s/ LEX v/s NEU	-	-	-	-	-	✓

Table 2: Comparison of formulations proposed by prior work on bias detection using BASIL, showing the different class combinations adopted for training. In the table, work by Fan et al. (2019) is denoted as 'Fan', van den Berg and Markert (2020) as 'Berg', (Lee et al., 2021) as 'Lee', Guo and Zhu (2022b) as 'Guo', and Lei et al. (2022) as 'Lei'.

informational bias as **'INF'**, sentences annotated with lexical bias as **'LEX'**. Additionally, we refer to the combination of neutral sentences with and sentences with lexical bias as **'OTH'**, while 'BIAS' refers to the combination of samples that have both informational and lexical bias.

Using the above definitions, we proceeded to analyze the settings proposed by previous work by Fan et al. (2019), van den Berg and Markert (2020), Lee et al. (2021), Guo and Zhu (2022b), and Lei et al. (2022) which we summarize in Table 2, above. We can see that there is a clear disparity in the way in which the bias detection tasks are approached. We further observe that detection of informational bias strikes as being the main focus in literature so far. We surmise that this issue may be due to the fact that lexical bias samples on BASIL appear to be considerably fewer than informational bias. However, we think that detection of lexical bias (Zhou and Bansal, 2020) should be at least as important as informational bias. While previous results focus mainly on the INF-related settings, we propose to experiment on classifying LEX bias from INF as, depicted in the first row of Table 2. To the best of our knowledge, no prior work on BASIL tried to make such a distinction. The relevance of our approach is evidenced by Chen et al. (2020), who showed that the detection of both INF and LEX bias together is difficult, with bias detection becoming harder at the article level.

In light of these observations, our work shows the results of several experiments we perform to compare and distinguish different bias in BASIL, using various settings. To further study the relationship between labels, we also propose a novel three-way classification approach to directly differentiate informational, lexical and neutral samples (INF/ LEX/ NEU), respectively.

As a result of our extensive study, we note that in many cases, performance gaps are due to lack of annotated examples for a given label, with this being particularly the case for lexical bias. In light of this issue, in this paper, we also adapt backtranslation as a mechanism for selective data augmentation in bias detection and use Google Translate python API for backtranslation. Our approach is inspired by previous work of Ma and Li (2020), who proposed a Chinese text data augmentation based on back-translation to generate a corpus to enrich the lexical features of text data, and reported increased performance on text classification tasks, especially when training on smaller datasets. Back-translation is also a commonplace to improve the performance on machine translation tasks (Miyabe and Yoshino, 2015). Our idea is also motivated by seminal work by Mikolov et al. (2013) who achieved 90% precision for translation of words between English and Spanish and found word vectors of both languages contain similar geometric arrangements. We used Google Translate python API which is accessible free under the MIT License.

Finally, we note that data preparation plays a significant role in machine learning, especially for natural language processing tasks (Marinov and Efremov, 2019). Inspired by the work by Zainol et al. (2018) and Ladani and Desai (2020), we **preprocess** sentences in the BASIL dataset to remove noise. Our proposed text preprocessing strategy involves two steps, first the removal of special characters and stop words i.e., words like 'after', 'before', 'the', 'some', 'all', 'such', and second reduction of words into their grammatical root or stem. In the context of bias classification task, as well shown in Section 5 we found that reducing the number of dimensions in terms of space (Rakholia and Saini, 2016) by removing most common words or words that normally carry no meaning has significant impact on bias detection.

4 Experimental Framework

In this section, we discuss the experimental framework including the setup, baselines, implementation details and give details of the models we train.

4.1 Setup

Backtranslation is performed separately on lexical and informational bias samples with one extra example per original (one half original and other half translated), hence doubling the size of lexical bias sentences to 956 samples and informational bias sentences to 2,498 samples respectively. Naturally, our backtranslation-based augmentation is performed only on the training set, with validation and testing always containing the original data samples

Our backtranslation approach is applied on the specific label of interest. For example, for the INF v/s LEX task, augmentation is only performed on lexical bias samples; while in INF v/s LEX v/s NEU task augmentation is performed on both lexical and informational bias samples, whereas no augmentation is performed on neutral sentences in all of of our experiments including this. INF v/s LEX v/s NEU task represent bias detection of whole BASIL corpus data, with neutral samples included. In the task INF v/s OTH, augmentation is only performed on informational bias sentences, where OTH represents the combination of lexical bias and neutral sentences.

We note that other kinds of splits exist for BASIL. Specifically, we find "story splits" by van den Berg and Markert (2020), also exist, where context is created by integrating events and articles. However, our work focuses on sentence classification without access to more context, and thus we report results on the traditional splits to retain consistency. Similarly, our testing data has no augmented example.

4.2 Baselines

Several deep learning approaches for the detection of bias in media have been proposed in previous work. Most of this work focuses on the detection of informational bias, and is based on the fine-tuning of large pre-trained models. In this paper, we concretely consider the informational bias detection approach by Fan et al. (2019), who proposed BERT-based (Devlin et al., 2018) approach and TF-IDF for this.

We also consider several models proposed by van den Berg and Markert (2020), which are used to detect informational bias in different ways. For starters, we compare with their BERT-based model as well as with their RoBERTa-based model Liu et al. (2019b). We also consider WinSCC (windowed Sequential Sentence Classification) which is a variant of SSC Cohan et al. (2019), ArtCIM (Article Context-Inclusive Model) and EvCIM (Event Context-Inclusive Model). We note that ArtCIM

Model	Aug.	Preproc.	INF/ LEX			INF/ LEX / NEU				INF/ OTH		
			Acc	F1-score		Acc	F1-score			Acc	F1-score	
				INF	LEX		INF	LEX	NEU		INF	OTH
BERT	-	-	74.46%	0.573	0.342	79.57%	0.383	0.194	0.880	76.55%	0.404	0.881
	-	✓	76.69%	0.687	0.534	77.78%	0.377	0.309	0.895	80.14%	0.423	0.871
	✓	-	81.37%	0.667	**0.691**	77.56%	**0.432**	**0.417**	0.864	81.53%	0.463	0.868
	✓	✓	**83.97%**	**0.712**	0.678	**81.54%**	0.429	0.401	**0.881**	**83.86%**	**0.507**	**0.899**
LSTM	-	-	72.63%	0.512	0.348	74.88%	0.301	0.209	0.856	73.93%	0.311	0.855
	-	✓	70.24%	0.594	0.432	71.34%	0.277	0.187	0.869	76.09%	0.332	0.823
	✓	-	70.01%	0.677	0.655	73.76%	0.319	**0.456**	**0.873**	75.34%	0.360	**0.875**
	✓	✓	**75.34%**	**0.692**	**0.671**	**75.56%**	**0.325**	0.450	0.851	**78.89%**	**0.381**	0.868
SVM	✓	✓	70.98%	0.491	0.795	74.23%	0.212	0.346	0.877	81.72%	0.178	0.890

Table 3: Results of our ablation study to understand the performance impact of our proposed backtranslation and data preprocessing approaches on three task formulations. In the Table, 'Aug.' denotes the usage of our augmentation techniques, while 'Preproc.' denotes models that included our preprocessing appraoch. We note that no prior work has done for the detection of the first two tasks we consider (INF v/s LEX and INF v/s LEX v/s NEU).

Model	INF / NEU		BIAS / NEU		LEX / NEU		INF / OTH	
	Acc	INF F1	Acc	BIAS F1	Acc	LEX F1	Acc	INF F1
TF-IDF (Fan et al., 2019)	-	26.02	-	-	-	-	-	-
BERT (Fan et al., 2019)	-	43.27	-	-	-	31.49	-	-
RoBERTa (Lee et al., 2021)	-	-	72.80	65.50	-	-	-	-
UnifiedM2 (Lee et al., 2021)	-	-	81.00	**70.20**	-	-	-	-
BERT (van den Berg and Markert, 2020)	-	-	-	-	-	-	-	38.26
RoBERTa (van den Berg and Markert, 2020)	-	-	-	-	-	-	-	49.89
WinSSC (van den Berg and Markert, 2020)	-	-	-	-	-	-	-	38.67
ArtCIM (van den Berg and Markert, 2020)	-	-	-	-	-	-	-	42.80
EvCIM (van den Berg and Markert, 2020)	-	-	-	-	-	-	-	44.10
MultiCTX Guo and Zhu (2022b)	-	-	-	-	-	-	-	46.08
RoBERTa Lei et al. (2022)	-	-	-	-	-	-	-	46.47
BERT (Ours)	**87.00**	**49.60**	**82.34**	69.00	**95.70**	**62.30**	**83.86**	**50.70**

Table 4: Comparison with previous work on four bias tasks using our BERT model. Results of our BERT on INF v/s NEU with augmentation of only informational bias, BIAS v/s NEU with augmentation of both informational and lexical bias, LEX v/s NEU with augmentation of only lexical bias, and INF v/s OTH with augmentation of only informational bias, respectively. BERT (Ours) report averaged results of three seed runs on all bias tasks. In the Table, 'Acc' denotes accuracy and only one prior work on task BIAS v/s NEU (Lee et al., 2021) reported accuracy.

and EvCIM integrate article and event context respectively and use BiLSTM's (Hochreiter and Schmidhuber, 1997) for bias detection. We also consider MultiCTX, as proposed by Guo and Zhu (2022b), which is based on contrastive learning on triplets sampled from different articles. We compare another model by Lei et al. (2022) built on RoBERTa that incorporates global functional discourse structure and local rhetorical discourse relations for detecting bias.

We further compare our models with the binary classification of informational and lexical bias with a RoBERTa model fine-tuned by Lee et al. (2021), and with their proposed UnifiedM2 model. This is a comprehensive misinformation detection model that was trained on the concatenation of multiple misinformation domains into a single unified setup.

4.3 Implementation Details

Our models are mainly based on BERT, in particular the implementation from HuggingFace (Face, 2021). We fine-tune BERT on our augmented and preprocesed data, using learning rate of 5×10^{-5}, and batch sizes of 16 or 32. The maximum epoch count in our experiments reaches up to 15.

We additionally use a model based on a LSTM that receives the same data which is already preprocessed as described previously. For this LSTM, we use a hidden size dimension of 200, with embeddings based on GloVe (Pennington et al., 2014). Finally, we also propose a simple approach based on a linear kernel SVM where we pass preprocessed augmented training sentences to the model.

For all of our experiments, we use 80/10/10 split with non-overlapping samples for train-validation-test, respectively. We reported the average performance of our models using three seed runs in our experiments.

5 Results & Discussion

We begin by testing the impact of our proposed data augmentation and preprocessing approaches by running ablation studies on three task settings. We first consider the newly-introduced tasks of INF/ LEX and INF/ LEX/ NEU, in addition to the more standard INF/ OTH setting, which is generic and of particular interest in the prior work. We measure the impact of each component of our proposed work by repeating the experiments and dividing our ablation test into two steps. To study and measure the significance of our proposed components, we first experiment only with data augmentation (denoted as 'Aug.') which involves the backtranslation of samples with bias, which is followed by our preprocessing step (denoted as 'Preproc.') which includes data cleaning, removal of stop words and stemming. The evaluation criteria we used is accuracy as 'Acc' and F1-micro score separately on each class of the bias i.e, INF, LEX, NEU, and OTH as explained earlier.

From our literature review, as discussed in Section 3 we found that many potentially relevant task formulations were missing. We surmise this could be due to the scarcity problem of lexical bias samples in BASIL, with interest focusing on only informational bias. We therefore propose to tackle all relevant task formulations.

Concretely, as to the best of our knowledge there is no prior work done to classify lexical bias from informational, we believe we are the first to identify and report experiments on the tasks of INF/ LEX as binary classification, as well as INF/ LEX/ NEU, use a multi-class classification.

As shown in Table 3, we found that in these tasks considerable performance improvements is achieved when both data augmentation and preprocessing are applied. For the binary INF/ LEX, we found that just by augmenting lexical bias, we are able to attain excellent performance. An improved accuracy of 83.97% with INF F1-score of 0.712 is achieved as compared to LSTM and SVM when both data preprocessing and augmentation are applied. We also observe that the highest LEX F1-score of 0.691 is comparatively lower than informational bias in the INF/ LEX task. One possible reason for that is the larger class imbalance of lexical bias sentences, which persists even after augmentation of lexical bias samples —1,259 informational v/s 956 lexical bias sentences, respectively. Despite this we note that the F1-score of lexical bias detection still approach considerably high value suggesting lexical bias can be classified from informational bias when computed together. Similarly, we observe that our augmentation approach has a more significant impact in performance compared to our pre-processing technique. When augmentation is applied alone, it improves the LEX F1-score from 0.534 to 0.691 using BERT, and from 0.432 to 0.655 for the LSTM. While our preprocessing also consistently improve performance, the gains are not as dramatic as the ones provided by the data augmentation.

We further note that our three-way classification task INF/ LEX/ NEU follows a similar trend, with significant performance improvements due to our data augmentation technique. A sharp rise in accuracy is observed by inclusion of both augmentation and preprocessing, leading to an accuracy of 81.54% when using BERT.

While we believe our experiments clearly show the effectiveness of our data cleaning and augmentation approaches in detecting all kinds of bias in BASIL, it is also worth pointing out that there are some limitations to what these techniques can do. For example, we note that when we only use our preprocesing, a decline in accuracy from 79.57% to 77.78% and INF F1-score from 0.383 to 0.377 using BERT are observed, while for the LSTM accuracy drops from 74.88% to 71.34% with a drop in INF F1-score from 0.301 to 0.277. We believe a possible reason for this might be similar to what Wendland et al. (2021) observed on a similar experiment, where it was shown that stemming could lead to lower accuracy and F1 scores. Since data preparation plays a significant role in capturing the knowledge gaps of natural language processing tasks, our rigorous ablation analysis of the tasks in Table 3 support the hypothesis that improvements in the detection of both informational and lexical bias at the sentences can be improved by performing data augmentation based on backtranslation and by preprocessing the data using stemming.

From prior work on BASIL as discussed previously and as shown in Table 2, most of the attention has been given to detecting only informational bias, especially the task of INF/ OTH, namely to classify informational bias from a combination of neutral and lexical bias sentences, which prompts us to consider this task also for our ablation study. Since informational bias is more common and difficult to detect as found by Fan et al. (2019); Chen et al. (2020), we highlight this task for our ablation study to demonstrate the significance of our proposed methods and to provide uniform results while comparing it with other methods in further experimental work. From these results, we observe similar trends compared to the other tasks, again showing the effectiveness of our proposed approach, which leads our BERT-based model to obtain a maximum F1-score of 0.507.

Having established the effectiveness of our proposed techniques, we now move on to compare our models with previous work, as shown in Table 4. Concretely, we compare against our selection of baseline models on four different existing tasks formulations derived from BASIL. For the comparisons in this section, we use our best model for each task i.e., the BERT-based approach combined with both of our proposed components, as evident from Table 3. Similarly, as before, we report accuracy and F1-score of each of the class. However, due to lack of completeness in the evaluation metrics found in previous work, we are only able to compare F1-scores of the baseline models with our proposed approach, except in the case of BIAS/ NEU task, where some previous work also report accuracy.

The first task shown in Table 4, INF/ NEU or namely to detect informational bias from neutral sentences, is only performed by Fan et al. (2019). We could only compare INF F1-score of baseline models with our proposed approach and found an improvement of 15% with final score of 49.60 using our BERT model, which compares against the reported performance of 43.27 F1-score.

In our second binary task, BIAS/ NEU, we use the same model configurations as Lee et al. (2021) with a batch size of 32, a learning rate of 5×10^{-6} with 15 as a maximum epoch count. Here BIAS corresponds to the combination of informational and lexical bias sentences, while NEU symbolizes only neutral sentences, which therefore corresponds to detecting bias v/s no bias sentences irrespective of their type. In this task, the highest BIAS F1-score is reported by UnifiedM2, and though we see that our proposed BERT-based approach does not outperform this model, our results are competitive as we observe we attain a similar performance. Furthermore, we note that our results in this task indicate that small focused data augmentation techniques as ours could be nearly as effective as more complicated training procedures including many tasks, as the approach proposed by UnifiedM2.

To detect lexical bias alone from neutral sentences, we study the task of LEX/ NEU. As shown in Table 4, in this case, the only baseline available is the BERT model proposed by Fan et al. (2019). For this task, we perform data augmentation of only lexical bias sentences, and we can see that BERT-based model outperforms the baseline BERT resulting in almost doubled LEX F1-score improvement, with our model attaining an F1-score of 62.3, while for the baseline BERT the value is just 31.49. We note that although BERT is our best model choice on this setting in terms of F1-score, our LSTM outperforms our BERT in terms of accuracy, obtaining 86.64%.

Finally, we consider the task of INF/ OTH, where we find most of previous work has focused. Concretely, for this task, we compare our BERT-based model with six previous models from the literature. As can be seen, we find that our model is able to outperform all existing prior work, achieving the best performance in terms of with INF F1-score of 50.9. Our model is followed by the RoBERTa model fine-tuned by (van den Berg and Markert, 2020) with INF F1-score of 49.89, where RoBERTa by Lei et al. (2022) as third with 46.47 and MultiCTX follows in the fourth position with F1-score of only 46.08. We believe this indicates that our approach is also better at recognizing informational bias as a type of misinformation.

Furthermore, we note that for the INF/ OTH task, many of our considered baselines are based on pre-trained models similar to ours, such as BERT or RoBERTa. As our model is based fundamentally on the same deep learning model, we believe these results suggest that our augmentation and pre-processing approaches might work for those models also. This adds to our observations derived from Table 3, where we saw that combining the LSTM with our proposed approach leads to consistent improvements also.

6 Conclusion

This paper presents different techniques of phrasing bias to tackle media bias in new outlets. We propose an approach that relies on current neural network models to capture sentence level biased language. We defined how data augmentation is applicable to less frequent bias in news articles and measure the effect of its performance across different models. Human annotation is costly and conditions where obtaining new misinformation samples is difficult, our approach is significant to such real life cases. Since our proposed approach involves simple feature extraction techniques to tackle a particularly small and unbalanced biased dataset, we believe our work can be used to mitigate bias and improve the quality of the model's predictions in real-world scenarios. We identify some novel tasks in BASIL and our augmentation technique effectively detect informational and lexical bias sentences simultaneously, while also outperforming in other tasks. In our work, we incorporate different methods to process bias and illustrate the importance of our proposed components. A key distinguishing feature of our work is the removal of inconsistencies of prior work in reporting and evaluating bias types of BASIL. Ablation studies are also performed by varying training data in different tasks and our technique suggest significance of each proposed component in different experimental settings. We found the performance improvement of our proposed approach in almost all tasks as compared to several state-of-the-art techniques, hence this proves that our methodological standpoint in using small augmented data is well-aligned in finding informational and lexical bias sentences in different classification tasks. Similarly, our work tries to propose a way of regulating different task formulations of BASIL which are unclear in prior work. We intend to explore context in BASIL news articles as future work, besides trying other feature selection techniques. We believe further parameter optimization and fine-tuning for different task formulations can also improve the results.

Limitations

One major limitation of our work is that we only experimented on an English dataset. While other lexical and syntactic features can be captured by text processing techniques and also backtranslation performed with other or multiple languages can be used to see the effect on performance. Other English news articles may also be useful for analyzing bias, and require further research analysis to verify media bias. Similarly, though our proposed approach works well for detecting bias in BASIL, we provide no evidence to suggest if this will also work on other misinformation-related tasks. The same applies for models other than the ones we tested in this paper, which though includes a broad selection (SVMs, LSTMs and Transformers) is not completely comprehensive.

Ethical Considerations

The interpretation of bias detection results is crucial. For cases, where different political entities are debatable in news media, may mislead the bias detection model and removing such bias require more flexible and tolerating approach while dealing with such entities. Therefore, the results reported in our work highlight the need for mitigating bias and further research is required to investigate the biased influence towards particular issues at various stages of the training model.

Acknowledgements

The authors wish to express gratitude to the funding organisation as this work has been supported by the Mohammed bin Salman Center for Future Science and Technology for Saudi-Japan Vision 2030 at The University of Tokyo (MbSC2030).

References

Dan Bernhardt, Stefan Krasa, and Mattias Polborn. 2008. Political polarization and the electoral effects of media bias. *Journal of Public Economics*, 92(5-6):1092–1104.

Marenglen Biba and Eva Gjati. 2014. Boosting text classification through stemming of composite words. In *Recent Advances in Intelligent Informatics*, pages 185–194. Springer.

Wei-Fan Chen, Khalid Al-Khatib, Benno Stein, and Henning Wachsmuth. 2020. Detecting media bias in news articles using gaussian bias distributions. *arXiv preprint arXiv:2010.10649*.

Arman Cohan, Iz Beltagy, Daniel King, Bhavana Dalvi, and Dan Weld. 2019. Pretrained language models for sequential sentence classification. In *Proceedings of the 2019 Conference on Empirical Methods in Natural Language Processing and the 9th International Joint Conference on Natural Language Processing (EMNLP-IJCNLP)*. Association for Computational Linguistics.

Aprillette Devanadera and Ericson Alieto. 2019. Noun bias among tagalog-speaking filipino pre-school children. *Devanadera, A., & Alieto, E.(2019). Lexical Bias among Tagalog-speaking Filipino Pre-school Children. Asian EFL*, 24(4.1):207–225.

Jacob Devlin, Ming-Wei Chang, Kenton Lee, and Kristina Toutanova. 2018. Bert: Pre-training of deep bidirectional transformers for language understanding. *arXiv preprint arXiv:1810.04805*.

John Duggan and Cesar Martinelli. 2011. A spatial theory of media slant and voter choice. *The Review of Economic Studies*, 78(2):640–666.

Sergey Edunov, Myle Ott, Michael Auli, and David Grangier. 2018. Understanding back-translation at scale. In *Proceedings of the 2018 Conference on Empirical Methods in Natural Language Processing*, pages 489–500, Brussels, Belgium. Association for Computational Linguistics.

Hugging Face. 2021. The ai community building the future. *URL: https://huggingface. co*.

Lisa Fan, Marshall White, Eva Sharma, Ruisi Su, Prafulla Kumar Choubey, Ruihong Huang, and Lu Wang. 2019. In plain sight: Media bias through the lens of factual reporting. In *Proceedings of the 2019 Conference on Empirical Methods in Natural Language Processing and the 9th International Joint Conference on Natural Language Processing (EMNLP-IJCNLP)*, pages 6343–6349, Hong Kong, China. Association for Computational Linguistics.

Stephan Greene and Philip Resnik. 2009. More than words: Syntactic packaging and implicit sentiment. In *Proceedings of Human Language Technologies: The 2009 Annual Conference of the North American Chapter of the Association for Computational Linguistics*, pages 503–511, Boulder, Colorado. Association for Computational Linguistics.

Shijia Guo and Kenny Q. Zhu. 2022a. Modeling multi-level context for informational bias detection by contrastive learning and sentential graph network.

Shijia Guo and Kenny Q Zhu. 2022b. Modeling multi-level context for informational bias detection by contrastive learning and sentential graph network. *arXiv preprint arXiv:2201.10376*.

Felix Hamborg, Karsten Donnay, and Bela Gipp. 2019. Automated identification of media bias in news articles: an interdisciplinary literature review. *International Journal on Digital Libraries*, 20(4):391–415.

Sepp Hochreiter and Jürgen Schmidhuber. 1997. Long short-term memory. *Neural computation*, 9(8):1735–1780.

Dirk Hovy and Shrimai Prabhumoye. 2021. Five sources of bias in natural language processing. *Language and Linguistics Compass*, 15(8):e12432.

Jeremy Howard and Sebastian Ruder. 2018. Universal language model fine-tuning for text classification. In *Proceedings of the 56th Annual Meeting of the Association for Computational Linguistics (Volume 1: Long Papers)*, pages 328–339, Melbourne, Australia. Association for Computational Linguistics.

Christoph Hube and Besnik Fetahu. 2019. Neural based statement classification for biased language. In *Proceedings of the Twelfth ACM International Conference on Web Search and Data Mining*. ACM.

Mohit Iyyer, Peter Enns, Jordan Boyd-Graber, and Philip Resnik. 2014. Political ideology detection using recursive neural networks. In *Proceedings of the 52nd Annual Meeting of the Association for Computational Linguistics (Volume 1: Long Papers)*, pages 1113–1122, Baltimore, Maryland. Association for Computational Linguistics.

Qiong Jia, Yue Guo, and Stuart Barnes. 2019. Understanding information bias: The perspective of online review component: An abstract. In *Academy of Marketing Science Annual Conference*, pages 157–158. Springer.

Anjali Ganesh Jivani et al. 2011. A comparative study of stemming algorithms. *Int. J. Comp. Tech. Appl*, 2(6):1930–1938.

Jessica L Johnson, Donna Adkins, and Sheila Chauvin. 2020. A review of the quality indicators of rigor in qualitative research. *American journal of pharmaceutical education*, 84(1).

Dhara J Ladani and Nikita P Desai. 2020. Stopword identification and removal techniques on tc and ir applications: A survey. In *2020 6th International Conference on Advanced Computing and Communication Systems (ICACCS)*, pages 466–472. IEEE.

Nayeon Lee, Belinda Z. Li, Sinong Wang, Pascale Fung, Hao Ma, Wen-tau Yih, and Madian Khabsa. 2021. On unifying misinformation detection. In *Proceedings of the 2021 Conference of the North American Chapter of the Association for Computational Linguistics: Human Language Technologies*, pages 5479–5485, Online. Association for Computational Linguistics.

Yuanyuan Lei, Ruihong Huang, Lu Wang, and Nick Beauchamp. 2022. Sentence-level media bias analysis informed by discourse structures. In *Proceedings of the 2022 Conference on Empirical Methods in Natural Language Processing*, pages 10040–10050.

Nelson F. Liu, Matt Gardner, Yonatan Belinkov, Matthew E. Peters, and Noah A. Smith. 2019a. Linguistic knowledge and transferability of contextual representations.

Yinhan Liu, Myle Ott, Naman Goyal, Jingfei Du, Mandar Joshi, Danqi Chen, Omer Levy, Mike Lewis, Luke Zettlemoyer, and Veselin Stoyanov. 2019b. Roberta: A robustly optimized bert pretraining approach. *arXiv preprint arXiv:1907.11692*.

Jun Ma and Langlang Li. 2020. Data augmentation for chinese text classification using back-translation. In *Journal of Physics: Conference Series*, volume 1651, page 012039. IOP Publishing.

Malini Mahendra, Yanting Luo, Hunter Mills, Gundolf Schenk, Atul J Butte, and R Adams Dudley. 2021. Impact of different approaches to preparing notes for analysis with natural language processing on the performance of prediction models in intensive care. *Critical care explorations*, 3(6).

Martin Marinov and Alexander Efremov. 2019. Representing character sequences as sets : A simple and intuitive string encoding algorithm for nlp data cleaning. In *2019 IEEE International Conference on Advanced Scientific Computing (ICASC)*, pages 1–6.

Tomas Mikolov, Quoc V Le, and Ilya Sutskever. 2013. Exploiting similarities among languages for machine translation. *arXiv preprint arXiv:1309.4168*.

Mai Miyabe and Takashi Yoshino. 2015. Evaluation of the validity of back-translation as a method of assessing the accuracy of machine translation. In *2015 International Conference on Culture and Computing (Culture Computing)*, pages 145–150. IEEE.

Pinelopi Papalampidi, Frank Keller, and Mirella Lapata. 2019. Movie plot analysis via turning point identification. In *Proceedings of the 2019 Conference on Empirical Methods in Natural Language Processing and the 9th International Joint Conference on Natural Language Processing (EMNLP-IJCNLP)*, pages 1707–1717, Hong Kong, China. Association for Computational Linguistics.

Jeffrey Pennington, Richard Socher, and Christopher D Manning. 2014. Glove: Global vectors for word representation. In *Proceedings of the 2014 conference on empirical methods in natural language processing (EMNLP)*, pages 1532–1543.

Rajnish M Rakholia and Jatinderkumar R Saini. 2016. Lexical classes based stop words categorization for gujarati language. In *2016 2nd international conference on advances in computing, communication, & automation (ICACCA)(Fall)*, pages 1–5. IEEE.

Marta Recasens, Cristian Danescu-Niculescu-Mizil, and Dan Jurafsky. 2013. Linguistic models for analyzing and detecting biased language. In *Proceedings of the 51st Annual Meeting of the Association for Computational Linguistics (Volume 1: Long Papers)*, pages 1650–1659, Sofia, Bulgaria. Association for Computational Linguistics.

Rico Sennrich, Barry Haddow, and Alexandra Birch. 2015. Improving neural machine translation models with monolingual data. *arXiv preprint arXiv:1511.06709*.

Sam Shleifer. 2019. Low resource text classification with ulmfit and backtranslation. *arXiv preprint arXiv:1903.09244*.

Connor Shorten, Taghi M Khoshgoftaar, and Borko Furht. 2021. Text data augmentation for deep learning. *Journal of big Data*, 8(1):1–34.

Jasmeet Singh and Vishal Gupta. 2016. Text stemming: Approaches, applications, and challenges. *ACM Computing Surveys (CSUR)*, 49(3):1–46.

Tony Sun, Andrew Gaut, Shirlyn Tang, Yuxin Huang, Mai ElSherief, Jieyu Zhao, Diba Mirza, Elizabeth Belding, Kai-Wei Chang, and William Yang Wang. 2019. Mitigating gender bias in natural language processing: Literature review. *arXiv preprint arXiv:1906.08976*.

Esther van den Berg and Katja Markert. 2020. Context in informational bias detection. In *Proceedings of the 28th International Conference on Computational Linguistics*, pages 6315–6326, Barcelona, Spain (Online). International Committee on Computational Linguistics.

André Wendland, Marco Zenere, and Jörg Niemann. 2021. Introduction to text classification: impact of stemming and comparing tf-idf and count vectorization as feature extraction technique. In *European Conference on Software Process Improvement*, pages 289–300. Springer.

Stephane Wolton. 2019. Are biased media bad for democracy? *American Journal of Political Science*, 63(3):548–562.

Tae Yano, Philip Resnik, and Noah A Smith. 2010. Shedding (a thousand points of) light on biased language. In *Proceedings of the NAACL HLT 2010 Workshop on Creating Speech and Language Data with Amazon's Mechanical Turk*, pages 152–158.

Zuraini Zainol, Mohd TH Jaymes, and Puteri NE Nohuddin. 2018. Visualurtext: a text analytics tool for unstructured textual data. In *Journal of Physics: Conference Series*, volume 1018, page 012011. IOP Publishing.

Xiang Zhou and Mohit Bansal. 2020. Towards robustifying nli models against lexical dataset biases. *arXiv preprint arXiv:2005.04732*.

Author Index

Bernacchia, Alberto, 17

DeHaven, Mitchell, 58

Ennen, Philipp, 17

Freddi, Federica, 17

Gales, Mark, 49
Grimminger, Lara, 29
Guzman Olivares, Daniel, 38

Klinger, Roman, 29
Kung, Po-Nien, 17

Lefebvre, Clément, 1
Liberatore, Federico, 38
Lin, Chyi-Jiunn, 17
Liusie, Adian, 49

Maab, Iffat, 66
Marrese-Taylor, Edison, 66
Matsuo, Yutaka, 66

Quijano, Lara, 38

Raina, Vatsal, 49

Scott, Stephen, 58
Shiu, Da-shan, 17
Stoehr, Niklas, 1

Wang, RenChu, 17
Wuehrl, Amelie, 29

Yang, Chien-Yi, 17

Association for Computational Linguistics
209 N. Eighth Street
Stroudsburg, Pennsylvania 18360

CURRAN ASSOCIATES INC. proceedings.com

ISBN 978-1-7138-7381-5